SOCCER

SKILLS & TACTICS

SOCCER

SKILLS & TACTICS

Glenn Moore

PARRAGON

First published in Great Britain in 1997 by
Parragon
13 Whiteladies Road
Clifton, Bristol BS8 1PB
United Kingdom

Reprinted in 1998

ISBN: 0-75252-692-8

Conceived, designed and produced by Haldane Mason, London

Acknowledgements
Art Director: Ron Samuels
Editor: Tessa Rose
Designer: Zoë Mellors
Picture Research: Charles Dixon-Spain

Colour reproduction by Regent Publishing Services, Hong Kong

Printed in Italy

Picture Acknowledgements
All Sport: 8 (top), 9 (top & bttm), 10, 11 (centre), 16–17, 19 (inset), 20–21, 21 (inset), 22–23, 23 (top), 24, 26–27, 26 (bttm), 28 (inset), 30, 31, 32, 32–33, 34, 35, 36–37, 37, 38–39, 39, 40 (top), 40 (inset), 40–41, 42–43, 44, 46–47 (all), 48–49, 51 (both), 52 (both), 54 (both), 55 (both), 56 (top), 57 (both), 58 (top), 59 (bttm), 63 (top), 65 (top), 69, 72, 73 (bttm), 74, 76 (top), 87 (bttm), 89, 90 (top), 91 (top), 92 (top)
Colorsport: 1, 2–3, 7, 12–13, 14 (both), 18–19, 25, 28–29, 45, 50 (bttm), 53 (both), 60 (bttm), 61 (both), 64 (bttm), 66 (both), 82, 83 (top right), 84 (all), 85 (all), 86, 88 (top), 90 (inset), 91 (bttm), 92 (bttm), 93 (all), 94 (both), 95 (top)
Sporting Pictures: 58 (bttm), 59 (top), 64 (top), 83 (top left & bttm), 88 (bttm)

Every effort has been made to trace the copyright holders and we apologize in advance for any unintentional errors or omissions. We would be pleased to insert the appropriate acknowledgement in any subsequent edition of this publication.

Contents

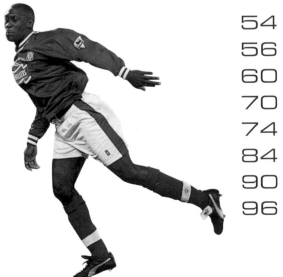

Foreword
By Terry Venables

When he was my player at Tottenham, Paul Gascoigne was not a great believer in tactics. Like many talented footballers he thought that as he was a good player he just had to go out and perform to his potential to do well. Most of the time in England that was true.

But when Paul went to Lazio, it was different. Opponents were more tactically aware. Soon after I became England coach, I went to see him play against Milan. Lazio struggled to make any impact on a well-organized Milan defence. Afterwards, Paul said he now realized why tactics were important. Despite all his skill, and that of his team-mates, Lazio had not got near the goal.

Paul was not alone. It is only recently, after several years of bad results in Europe, that the English game has accepted that it needs to become more tactically sophisticated. There has also been a realization that, while we have talented players like Paul Gascoigne, we are generally less skilful than foreign teams. Our technical inferiority did not matter when we were stronger and fitter, but now that many countries can match our traditional strengths we have to be able to match theirs.

This book is thus a timely addition to the football library. I got to know its author, Glenn Moore, when he was reporting on the England team for the *Independent*. The journalists who cover football at that level are in a position of considerable influence and we managers often wonder what right they have to judge us. Glenn has more right than most because he has experienced an integral part of our work. He has stood there in front of a class and qualified as a coach. This is not everything, but it does take away the core criticism we have of journalists.

It would help if all of them did it. The more knowledge journalists, players, spectators – and coaches, for we are always learning – have of the game, the more it will be understood and appreciated.

Introduction

Whether you are Eric Cantona, being banned for eight months, or Joe Bloggs, conceding six goals on a cold February day in Hackney, there will be times when you wonder why you ever took up football. Then you will recall other moments, which you will remember for ever – lifting the FA Cup at Wembley, or scoring the last-minute goal that clinched the Hackney Marshes Third Division title.

Soccer, association football, fussball, voetbal, or whatever it is called in your part of the world, is the most popular game on the planet. It is not hard to understand why – you do not have to be particularly tall or strong to play, nor do you have to be quick in movement or thought. All these attributes help, but all can be overcome. A game can be two children kicking a ragball about on a dusty patch of waste ground in Africa, or 22 highly paid professionals playing in front of an audience of millions in a World Cup final. Football offers something to everybody.

Whatever level you play at, or watch, your enjoyment can be increased by being better informed about how to play the game. The aim of this book is to do that, whether you are a boy with dreams of greatness; a Sunday park player who has finally accepted that Liverpool are never going to realize their talents; or a spectator who wants to better appreciate the skills seen on a Saturday afternoon – or whenever your team plays these days.

'You are never too old to learn' may be a cliché but it is still true. I was 32 when I did my FA coaching course and it taught me a great many things I wish I had learned at the age of 12. What I discovered benefits me, whether I'm covering a scintillating European Cup tie at Old Trafford, or a badly positioned team-mate in the Leatherhead & District League.

Writing a book, like playing football, is best achieved as part of a team and I am grateful for the help of several team-mates in getting this project on to the bookshelves.

Special thanks are due to Terry Venables, both for kindly taking time out from a busy schedule to write the foreword and for his encouragement. Thanks also to Ken Jones, a respected colleague on the *Independent* and a former professional player, who generously read through the manuscript and made several useful suggestions. Any remaining errors and omissions are mine, not Terry's or Ken's.

Thank you also to the team at Haldane Mason – Tessa, Syd, Charlie and Ron – for their support and advice. The excellent look of the book is down to them.

Last, but definitely not least, many thanks to my fiancée, Claire, for putting up with the hours I've spent writing, typing and reading for the book. Thanks, in particular, for her tolerance during what was supposed to be a week's holiday.

Much of this book has come from my own observations and conversations but, inevitably, I have also drawn from several sources. These include: *The Umbro Book of Football Quotations* by Phil Shaw and Peter Ball; *The Winning Formula* by Charles Hughes (I don't agree with the statistics or the philosophy, but there is still

Eric Cantona enjoys one of football's peak experiences – lifting the FA Cup in May 1996.

much to recommend), *Learn Football with Jack Charlton* by Jack Charlton (good for children), and *Soccer Techniques, Tactics & Teamwork* by Gerhard Bauer (for advanced players and coaches).

If you are seeking to improve your play, reading this book will not be enough. Just as low-fat meals only help you lose weight as part of a calorie-controlled diet, this book will only make you a better player if you accompany it with practice – and plenty of it. And whether you are practising, playing or watching, try and ensure – as all the great managers are supposed to have said – that you 'go out there and enjoy it'.

Glenn Moore
London, 1997

Preparation

Football is one of the easiest games in the world to play. At its simplest it is just a matter of finding a bit of spare land and a vaguely spherical object. Many a mother could call a pair of scuffed school shoes as witness to the fact that most of us have, at some time, played with taped bundles of newspaper, golf balls, conkers, even a tin can.

Equipment

Gianluca Vialli warms up for action.

But, like most sports, football has become big business and the further you progress the greater the choice of equipment. Some football boots have fins and wedges that are supposed to make the ball swerve and dip in flight. They do, but only if you can play like Robbie Fowler. For most players, using one of these boots is just like using one of the modern golf balls that travel further than ever – they make a bad shot worse.

Boots should be chosen for comfort, not because your favourite player gets a lucrative modelling contract to wear them. It is not unknown for players to wear a different make of boot and decorate them in the logo of their sponsor. If you are not happy in your boots, you will not play well. Buying boots that are too large so you can 'grow into them' is usually a mistake, because they cause blisters and affect your 'feel' for the ball.

The second key element is grip. If you can afford it, have long studded boots for wet pitches in November, short studs for hard grounds in August and pimpled ones for frozen February and artificial surfaces. However, for most conditions one pair of screw-ins, with various-sized studs, is sufficient, plus trainers for artificial pitches.

Boots have improved considerably in recent years but new ones may still cause blisters. Vaseline on the heel and top-of-the-toe areas can ease that.

After use, boots should be dried naturally – not on a radiator. They will dry quicker, and keep their shape, if the ends are stuffed with newspaper. Remember to take the paper out after a day or two.

Shinpads are also vital – and are compulsory in many leagues. Buy a pair that combine comfort with strength. They should not be so bulky as to hinder movement, but they should be strong enough to enable you to tackle with confidence. Some provide heel protection as well.

Most other kit will be provided by organized teams. If possible wear cotton, especially on the feet – cotton/lambswool mixes can be found which reduce blisters and fungal infection through sweating.

Warming-up, fitness training, warming-down

Once you have a football at your feet, it is always tempting to start kicking it about. This is not advisable. Whatever sports activity you are about to undertake, a few minutes spent warming-up pays off.

English football has been slow to appreciate the importance of muscle flexibility, but the influence of coaches like Ruud Gullit and Arsene Wenger has increased awareness. Develop a routine that stretches all parts of the body, especially the areas that are placed under stress in a game: upper and lower legs (hamstring, groin, calf), stomach (abdominal) and side (intercostal) muscles and neck. Goalkeepers also need to play particular attention to shoulders and arms.

Stretch gradually and 'hold' the position for a few seconds. Do not 'bounce' or 'spring' the muscles. This should also be done before fitness training. Most players prefer kicking a ball to running, but fitness is increasingly vital. The fitter you are the greater

contribution you can make to a game. You will also make fewer mistakes – many a goal has been conceded near the end of a game because physical tiredness has induced mental tiredness.

It is better to exercise little but often than do a lot in one hit. Tailor your exercise to football – lots of short sprints as well as distance work. Try to use good running shoes and avoid too much running on concrete, especially if you usually play on artificial surfaces. Young players, who are more vulnerable to stress injuries, should not do as much endurance training as older ones; fortunately they have more natural stamina.

Weights should be used in moderation. Heavy muscle affects mobility. Do 'repetitions', lifting small weights many times, rather than lifting as much as possible a few times.

It is important to warm down after exercise. This is a shortened version of warming up. Doing so on a regular basis will gradually increase the flexibility of your muscles and prevent cramping.

Alan Shearer and David Beckham watch Paul Gascoigne practising during Euro 96.

Part I:
Developing
Skills

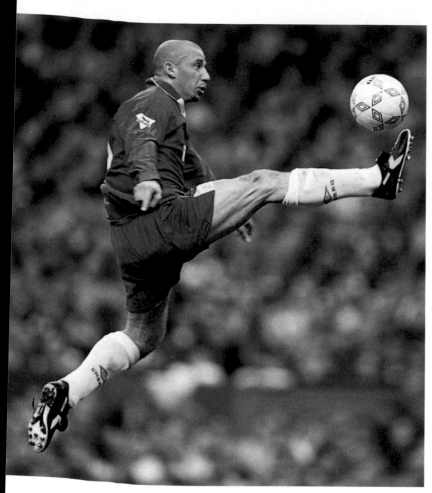

Football is all about possession of the ball. Without it, you cannot do anything, except run around trying to stop the opposition using it. With it, everything is possible. The ability to control the ball – trapping it, passing it, shooting with it – is thus the most prized in the game. In a 90-minute match the average player will actually be in possession of the ball for about three minutes so he, or she, may as well make the most of it.

Above: Vialli stretches to control the ball with confidence.
Right: Ryan Giggs hones his ball skills with this heel flick.

Practice may not make perfect but it can make permanent. The more an action is performed the more naturally it will come to a player under pressure.

Then there are the defensive arts.

Good tackling is a skill in itself, as is good goalkeeping. While keen to promote attacking football it is always worth remembering the maxim, 'if you don't concede a goal, you don't lose'.

I was right-footed to start with, but I worked harder on my left and it became better than my right. It annoys me today when I see players earning £32,000 a week who can't kick with both feet. I find it amazing that professionals can't do that.

George Best, 1996.

Passing

Passes are the glue that binds a team's play. They can be five yards or fifty, forwards, backwards or sideways. A good pass consists of two skills: selection and execution. The first requires judgement (of which type of pass to play and where to play it); the second, technique.

Teddy Sheringham, a fine long passer, points the way forward for England against Georgia.

Judgement comes from experience and awareness – of where team-mates are, of where opponents are, and of what is possible. Keep looking around, before you get the ball, so you already know where players are when it arrives. Gianfranco Zola is a good example of this.

If you can, pass forwards, but not aimlessly. If there is a high chance that the long forward ball will result in a loss of possession, pass sideways or backwards. The nearer you are to your own goal the more care is needed. Backpasses to the goalkeeper, or across your own goal, are

Passing while marked from behind

1 Be first to the ball and balanced to play it. You should already know where you intend to play it.

2 Keeping your body between the ball and your opponent, flick the ball to your team-mate.

risky and may result in a goalscoring chance for the opposition. Remember, all the time you have the ball the opposition cannot score. However, too much emphasis on possession can result in negative play and puts the ball at risk in dangerous areas. At times it may be worth playing a speculative long forward pass.

When passing it is vital to get the 'weight' right. Passes to the feet should be hit firmly but not so hard as to make control difficult. Passes to moving players should be made with their movement in mind – for example, quick forwards normally like the ball played into space behind the defence. Timing, playing the ball just before a forward steps offside rather than just after, and accuracy, without which all the preparation is usually wasted, are the final components of a successful pass.

While you are deciding where to pass, it is important not to let opponents get so close that they reduce your angle. Team-mates can help by opening up an angle for you to pass into.

The process of kicking the ball involves three facets. The approach during which posture needs to be right; the kick, during which the ball needs to be hit in the right area with appropriate power; and the follow-through which, in a well-balanced kick, comes naturally. Concentration needs to be maintained throughout – lazy passes are often inaccurate. The position of the standing foot is critical and cannot be over-emphasized.

In matches, pass with your better foot when possible, but practise with the weaker one. Being able to use both feet will significantly improve your effectiveness.

To someone who has not played much the following descriptions of how to pass correctly may seem daunting. They need not be: most actions will follow naturally once the basic movement is correct. With a little practice passes you once had to think about will become instinctive. More experienced players should not gloss over the next few pages – it is worth checking that you have not acquired bad habits, especially as most passing techniques also apply to shooting.

SIDE PASS

This is the most frequently used pass in football. It is the quickest and most accurate way of moving the ball over short distances. A team like Liverpool use it constantly, with John Barnes regularly involved, as they try to pass themselves into a position to open an opposing team's defence.

Approach:

Sometimes known as the 'push pass', this is usually played from a relatively stationary position. As with most passes the non-kicking foot is placed alongside the ball but with enough space to allow the kicking foot to swing freely from the hip. Both feet should be slightly flexed at the knee – power comes from the thigh. Both arms should be slightly away from the body to provide balance. The upper body and head are over the ball.

Execution:

The foot comes through horizontally a few inches above the ground at right angles to the non-kicking foot to meet the ball side-on.

Sometimes the inside of the foot can be used to steer a moving ball to either side. For a right-footed pass the body is opened out to play it to the right, or closed up to turn it to the left. Accuracy is harder to achieve with these passes.

INSTEP PASS

Once players have progressed beyond the 'toe-punt' stage, this is the most natural way of kicking the ball. In the 1980s, when English football leaned towards 'long-ball, direct-play' methods, it was often the most common form of passing. It is still the favoured method of shooting for goal and playing long passes, because it provides more power than any other method of striking the ball. David Beckham is probably the best practitioner of this skill in the English game today.

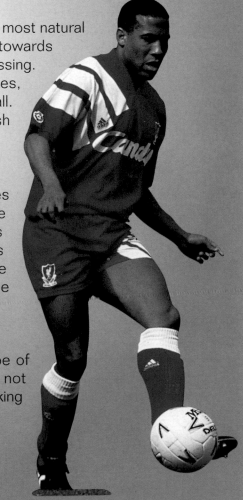

Approach:

Where possible, on the move from a slight angle. As with most passes the non-kicking foot should be aligned alongside the ball pointing in the intended direction of the pass or shot. To keep the ball down the eyes should be focused on the ball at the moment of impact – this ensures the head stays down. Arms are flung out for balance, especially on the non-kicking side, foot muscles are tightened just before impact and the leg swings from the knee.

Execution:

The ball is struck in the centre with the laces area of the boot. The toe of the boot should be pointing towards the ground but at a slight angle, not vertical. Power comes from the calf muscle – hit 'through' the ball. The kicking foot should follow through slightly across the body.

LOFTED INSTEP PASS

Used primarily for long kicks from defensive positions, crosses from deep, or corners, this pass has the advantage of bypassing opponents on the ground. Accuracy can be a problem on windy days. Players of the quality of Glenn Hoddle could play this pass and make the ball 'sit up' on landing, like a top golfer putting backspin on an iron shot.

Approach:

Similar to an instep pass but with the non-kicking foot alongside but slightly behind the ball and the body leaning backwards. The head goes up just before impact. To make the ball rise more steeply approach from a more angled approach. To get more power approach more directly.

Execution:

As for the instep pass, except you strike the lower part of the ball, not the middle. Follow-through is important.

CHIP PASS

As Peter Schmeichel discovered in 1996, the chip can be a devastating weapon. It can be scooped, or kicked. In shooting it punishes a goalkeeper for being too far off his line; in passing it is a very good method of by-passing the back-line from close range. The chip has a limited range but, played properly, produces backspin.

Approach:

Can be played either standing still, or coming onto the ball. The usual complements – head over the ball, arm on non-kicking side out for balance – apply. The non-kicking foot is adjacent to the ball.

Execution:

In most cases the kicking foot stabs down under the ball like a sand wedge shot in golf. An alternative is to lift the ball up with with a scooping motion – this method can only be played over very short distances and does not achieve back-spin. But it is rarely expected. With both types of chip, lift the knee at the moment of impact.

TIPS FROM THE COACH

A successful pass requires weight, timing and accuracy.

•

The position of the head and non-kicking foot is as important as the kicking foot.

•

Concentrate.

BACKHEEL

The backheel is one of the flashiest passes in a player's armoury – and also one of the most likely to concede possession. However, when played well it is devastatingly effective.

Approach:
Use in attacking areas of the pitch and in defensive areas only with extreme caution. Successful execution requires a strong awareness of the positions of other players, both team-mates' and opponents'.

Execution:
There are two techniques. One should be called the classic backheel because the back of the heel is used. This method has more power, but less accuracy, than simply rolling the ball backwards with the sole of the boot. The ball is usually directly under the body, which is upright.

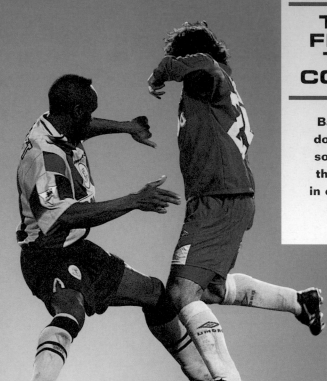

TIPS FROM THE COACH

Backheels do not look so clever if they result in conceding a goal.

OUTSIDE OF THE FOOT

This is more often a flick than a kick, especially when played by a closely marked forward to release a team-mate by deflecting a ball played up to them from midfield or defence. Also used as a quick method of laying off a ball to the side while on the move. Easy to disguise.

Approach:
The non-kicking foot is a little behind the ball. The knees are bent.

Execution:
The ball is struck with the outside of the foot between ankle and toe. The angle of the shot can be altered by turning the ankle as the ball is struck.

❝ Make it simple, make it accurate, make it quick. ❞

Arthur Rowe,
former manager of Spurs, on passing.

CHEST PASS

An ingenious pass that can keep play moving when defenders do not expect it. Ruud Gullit and Kenny Dalglish were masters of the art.

Approach and Execution:

The ball is received at any point between stomach and head level. By either bending knees, or jumping up, the player ensures the ball makes contact with the chest. He then 'bounces' the ball off his chest in the path of a team-mate.

The pass can be cushioned, by drawing back the chest at the moment of impact, or given extra distance by thrusting the chest out. Direction can be changed by turning the chest – this is particularly useful when seeking to release a team-mate running past while you are being closely marked.

HEAD PASS

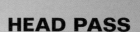

The head is a remarkably versatile passing tool. Andy Gray, the former Everton, Aston Villa, Wolves and Scotland striker, now a TV commentator, was one of those players who seemed to find it easier to pass with the head than the feet.

We will deal with heading techniques later. Just two golden rules will suffice here. If you can, head the ball while keeping your feet on the ground – it gives you better balance. And keep your eyes open.

Flick-on:

This also covers the glance, and the controlled deflection. When flicking on, say, at a corner, the ball should skim off the forehead. If you are in the right position, a slight back-flick, barely more than a raising of the eyebrows, should do the trick.

Other variations need more of a twist by the neck. For a stronger deflection – as used by a defender clearing the ball across his area, twist the body with the head. You should end up facing the direction you want the ball to go in.

Nod-down:

This is easier to control, the ball being steered into the path of a team-mate. This pass can be made with a 'nodding' motion, or cushioned, so the head draws back at the moment of impact, allowing the ball to fall gently to a team-mate close by.

Swerving the Ball

A difficult skill but an impressive one if mastered, both in look and effect. Many a brilliant goal has been scored with a 'Brazilian bender' and many created through a curving pass.

Inswing

Approach:
From the side with the non-kicking foot alongside and behind the ball. Both legs should be slightly bent at the knee, the arm on the non-kicking side out for balance.

Execution:
Strike the outside of the ball with the inside of your instep. The follow through should be straight.

Outswing

Approach:
Almost straight, legs slightly bent, arm on non-kicking side as balance. Lean slightly over the ball (but not too much if you want to lift it).

Execution:
Strike the inside of the ball with the outside of your foot. The follow-through should be across the body.

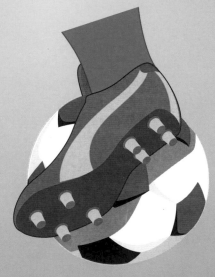

It used to be only during World Cup competitions that English audiences would see the ball swerving into the top corner from a free-kick. Now there are many British and Irish players who can bend the ball around defensive walls – Kevin Sheedy, Paul Gascoigne, Gary McAllister and Stuart Pearce are a few exponents who come to mind.

Free-kicks and corners (watch Andy Hinchcliffe) are the obvious uses of this skill, but it can also provide a devastating pass, notably inside the full-back. The principle is easy: hit the ball to one side, imparting spin or swerve. Execution is rather more tricky.

The kick can be made with the inside or outside of the foot. Accuracy is easier with the inside, power easier with the outside.

The ball swerves in the opposite direction to the side of the ball struck; i.e. hit the right side of the ball and it will curve to the left.

For the scientifically minded the technique is known as the 'Magnus effect' and it is achieved through the spin creating unequal air pressure around the ball, similar to a cricket spinner's use of 'flight'.

Incidentally, the lighter the ball, or the thinner the air, the easier it is to achieve (and the harder to control). Some balls swerve more than others; Arsenal players discovered in the mid-1990s that if you placed the ball used in the Premiership with the bladder valve facing the striker the ball would swerve sharper and later, like a Waqar Younis yorker in cricket.

Opposite: Dennis Bergkamp of Arsenal has his sights firmly set on the top right-hand corner of the goal as he bends the ball round the outside of the Manchester City wall.

Volleys

A technically difficult but spectacular skill, requiring balance, concentration, timing and athleticism. Volleying is used for shooting as much as passing because it can produce great power but variable accuracy. Mark Hughes of Wales, Manchester United and Chelsea is as good an exponent as any.

Any occasion when the ball is kicked while off the ground is a volley; when it is hit as it lands, it is a half-volley. Most volleys are hit with the instep; the differences are produced by the angle of the body during execution. The ankle is always extended: i.e. with the toe of the foot stretching out.

Upright volley

In general this is either a shot or a clearance. If it is a shot, the aim is to keep the ball down by getting head and knee over the ball, striking it late, and not following through. The ball should be hit about a foot, or 16 inches off the ground (30–40 cm).

For a clearance the body leans back, the ball is hit earlier and the leg follows through. The ball can be hit relatively comfortably from 1–2 feet (30–60 cm) off the ground.

A cross between the two is the volleyed lob in which the ball is gently lifted over the player in front, usually an advancing goalkeeper.

If the ball is rising (hitting it on the 'up'), you have to move very quickly into the shot to keep it down, almost throwing your body towards the ball. This was a speciality of Bobby Charlton, who scored many spectacular goals with this volley.

Above: **Paul Gascoigne shoots on the volley during Euro '96.**

Half-volley

Hard to keep down, you need to ensure that head and knee are over the ball. Although less powerful than a full volley, this shot can trouble goalkeepers, especially on difficult surfaces.

Sideways volley

This is played with the body side-on and the kicking leg extended horizontally (or within a few degrees, depending on the height of the ball). Get into position early and swivel on the non-kicking foot. The body leans back, both arms are flung out and the kicking foot comes up in an arc to meet the ball. To keep the ball down, turn your body into the ball and keep your head facing down. To lift the ball, raise your head at the moment of impact and lean back more.

For both types the kicking foot should follow through across the body and the non-kicking foot pivot to face the direction the ball has gone.

Flying sideways volley

Difficult to play and rarely used, this shot virtually invites a caution for dangerous play. Take off from the kicking foot, swivel in mid-air, and shoot with the instep while roughly

1 FLYING SIDEWAYS VOLLEY:
Having taken off with the kicking foot and twisted in mid-air, you should be in position to volley with the instep.

1 UPRIGHT VOLLEY:
When using this type of volley to shoot, as here, keep the ball down by ensuring that both head and knee are over the ball.

TIPS FROM THE COACH

Decide quickly how you are going to hit the ball and keep your eyes on it.

•

Strike the ball with the instep and follow through smoothly.

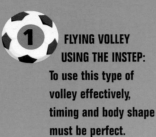 **FLYING VOLLEY USING THE INSTEP:** To use this type of volley effectively, timing and body shape must be perfect.

TIPS FROM THE COACH

Clever shots require great technical proficiency. Don't try them unless you are confident of playing them effectively.

•

Use such shots only where a simpler alternative is not available.

BICYCLE, OR SCISSORS, KICK: With this dramatic version of the overhead kick, the non-kicking foot should be thrown down for leverage, the head and back arched, and the ball struck with the instep.

horizontal. The non-kicking foot should also be near-horizontal but behind the kicking foot at the moment of impact. Sounds easy! Take care on landing.

Overhead kick

Can be played safely – as long as no opponent is close – with the non-kicking foot on the ground. It can be a useful way of clearing the ball. Played gently it can be a clever pass, though accuracy is difficult.

Bicycle kick

The dramatic version of the overhead kick, also known as the scissors kick, and a very effective way of making a surprise shot.

However, it is difficult to perform and risks being penalized in a crowded penalty area.

Take off from the kicking foot, swing the non-kicking foot down for leverage, throw the head back and arch your back as you try to hit the ball with the instep. Take care on landing.

Flick volley

The least powerful volley and the only one in which the ball is not hit with the instep. Played with either the inside or outside of the boot, it is a neat way of flicking the ball onto a team-mate behind and to the side. The non-kicking foot should remain on the ground and the body lean slightly back.

Eric Cantona volleys. Note his head position: he has watched the ball on to his foot.

Shooting

Think of football's most enduring moments: Geoff Hurst scoring England's fourth while Kenneth Wolstenholme proclaims 'they think it's all over – it is now'; Carlos Alberto scoring at the end of a stunning Brazilian move in another World Cup final; Paul Gascoigne scoring against Scotland in Euro 96 – they are all about shooting.

> **My strikers couldn't hit a donkey's arse with a frying pan.**
>
> **Dave Bassett, manager of Sheffield United, 1991.**

Goalkeeping is important, so is tackling, passing, dribbling – but without shots there would be no winners, no losers. Shooting is the most crucial art of all footballing skills, which is why the most famous players and expensive transfers, from Alf Common to Alan Shearer, have usually been forwards.

It is often said that great goalscorers are born not created. True, up to a point. Shearer, Gary Lineker, Robbie Fowler were all blessed with that predator's instinct, that penalty-box cool, which great strikers need. But they also worked very hard at their game. The lower the level the more that hard work and knowledge can make a difference.

Another quality they all had is the desire to score. It sounds obvious but many players will pass, or delay, rather than shoot. Great goalscorers are greedy, they believe they are more likely to score than anyone else on the pitch and, because they therefore have more shots than anyone else, they are usually right. Do not shoot when some-

one is obviously better placed, but be prepared to shoot whenever possible, even from long range – the goalkeeper could be unsighted, the ball might swerve. If you don't shoot you will never score. If you do, anything could happen – a goalkeeping error, a deflection, a lucky rebound . . . a goal. On the same theme, always support team-mates who have had a shot rather than criticize them, unless other forwards are obviously better placed.

And when you shoot, hit the target, make the goalkeeper work. The cardinal sin is to shoot over the bar – even a wide shot invites a fortuitous deflection.

Penalty-box poise comes from confidence which, usually, stems from goals. It can't be taught, but mental strength – the ability to believe in yourself during the bad spells – can.

This is important – when shooting, you need the confidence to choose the moment, and not rush your shot. When a goalkeeper approaches, try and force him to commit himself first. When shooting, aim either for the far post or low and close to the goalkeeper's legs. Those shots are difficult for him to save, while shots across the goal are more likely to rebound in front of the goal where a team-mate may be following up. There is also a greater chance of a deflection – think of Arsenal captain Tony Adams' goal in Highbury's North London derby in 1996/7 – it would have missed

Tim Breaker of West Ham.

the far post but went in off Sol Campbell.

That same game demonstrated another maxim – the importance of the first touch. Dennis Bergkamp's first touch set up Arsenal's third goal.

Bergkamp is a great example of another key principle when shooting – aim low. It is harder for a goalkeeper to save a ball at ground level than at waist or head height. Also, this increases the likelihood of the ball bouncing in front of him, and making it harder to catch.

One kick mainly used for shooting is the stab, almost a toe-poke. Kenny Dalglish was an expert at this – punting the ball forward while the goalkeeper waited for him to pull his foot back to shoot, or thought he had over-run. It can be poked under the keeper, or chipped over him, depending where contact is made with the ball.

Les Ferdinand of Newcastle shoots for goal.

Ball Control

'Get it under, GET. IT. UNDER. Agh no!'. It's a regular enough cry from supporters in the Premiership, let alone Sunday morning coaching sessions. Without ball control you can do very little. 'Touch' is all important, whether it is in preparation for a shot at goal, or bringing down a wayward pass from the opposition.

David Ginola controls the ball as Gary Neville watches.

This does not just mean being able to juggle the ball for hours, a very impressive skill but, as a veteran colleague of mine once said when watching such an exhibition at Wembley, 'I'd like to see him do that with someone kicking him'.

Control is a means to an end. So, when bringing the ball down, turning or dribbling with it, you should automatically be thinking of the next move and preparing for it. Ideally, control can be executed without looking at the ball so the head is up.

Trapping the Ball

The first action as the ball approaches is to assess where to receive it. Usually it is best to be in the line of flight, but sometimes an advantage can be gained from meeting the ball at an angle, so keeping the body between ball and opponent. The next decision is to determine which part of the body to control it with. This should take into account that you are going to meet the ball, not wait for it to come to you. If you wait, you lose time and could be dispossessed.

For most traps you relax your muscles at the moment you receive the ball, making them 'elastic'. For a few – the 'wedge' traps – you tense them as you do in most shooting and passing actions. Keep the head still.

Even as you receive the ball you should be planning your next step. This is usually one of gaining enough space to play in and can be done by trapping the ball to one side, rather than under your feet, and/or making

1 TRAPPING WITH THE OUTSIDE OF THE FOOT: Cover the ball with the outside of the foot as it lands and move away into space from your stationary foot.

1 TRAPPING WITH THE SIDE OF THE FOOT: The impact of the ball should be 'cushioned' by the trapping foot.

1 THE SOLE TRAP: Contact is made as the ball hits the ground, with the ball being 'wedged' under the foot to prevent it bouncing away.

TIPS FROM THE COACH

As the ball comes towards you, work out:

Which position you will take.

Which part of the body you will use.

What you will do when the ball is under control.

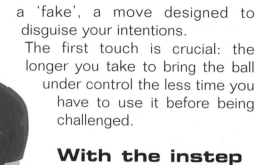

a 'fake', a move designed to disguise your intentions.

The first touch is crucial: the longer you take to bring the ball under control the less time you have to use it before being challenged.

With the instep

The most difficult of foot traps. The idea is to 'catch' the ball on the instep, or laces area, of the boot. Get into the line of flight and meet the ball with the foot raised and the toe pointing slightly upwards. Try to get your foot to 'give' with the momentum of the ball as you would with your hands when catching a 'skied' cricket ball.

Few players actually catch the ball on their foot but mimicking the motion will bring the ball down gently enough for you to play it.

With the sole

A basic trap with a wedge technique. Get in the line of flight and meet the ball as it hits the ground, trapping it under the sole of the foot with a gentle stamping action. Good for controlling a high ball but it can leave the ball under your feet. Timing is important – if you meet the ball too early, or too late, it will run away from you.

With the inside and outside of the foot

A similar trap but one which also deals with balls coming from either side and sets you up for the next move. To draw the ball across you, cover it with the inside of the foot as it lands and turn into the ball as you trap it. To move into space to the side, cover the ball with the outside of the foot as it lands and move off away from your stationary foot.

The stamping motion is less pronounced, and the trapping foot more relaxed, because the ball needs to be cushioned to draw the sting from the bounce.

With the shins

On wet surfaces it can be just as easy to trap the ball with the shins, bending the knees to provide a 'roof' for the trap. This trap is not advised if there is an opponent near by, because the ball can cannon away.

With the inside of the foot

This is the simplest trap. Receive the ball with the inside of the foot, between the heel and the big toe, gently cushioning the ball so it either stops dead or very close. The angle of the foot, which should be horizontal and a few inches off the ground, can be altered to change the direction you wish to play in. It can be helpful to receive the ball side-on in order to control it and turn in one movement.

Sometimes it is more convenient to trap the ball with the outside of the foot using the same principles.

With the thigh

The same principle of breaking the ball's motion is used in this trap. Get into the line of flight, bring your thigh up and, upon impact, drop it down. The higher up the thigh you receive the ball the easier it will be to control, because the tissue in this part of the body is softer.

The ball can be set up for a volley, by introducing an element of resistance, or dropped at your feet by relaxing the thigh muscles completely. It can also be steered to either side of the body by presenting the appropriate side of the thigh as you approach the ball.

Chest trap

Easier than it looks – and less painful. You have a large area to 'catch' the ball on, so the margin of error is good. Again, get into the line of flight and lean back to cushion the ball. It is easier with both feet on the ground but can be done in the air – Ruud Gullit is

THIGH TRAP:
With both this type of trap and the chest trap shown below the body needs to be cushioned to absorb the impact. The ball should fall to your feet.

CHEST TRAP:
This is easier than the thigh trap and less painful. Remember to keep your arms out of the way of the ball.

particularly adept at controlling the ball in this way.

Again, by turning your body you can steer the ball into the direction you wish to progress. Be careful to keep your arms out of the way.

By bending your knees you can chest trap the ball over a variety of heights. The chest can also control a difficult bouncing ball by smothering it 'on the up'.

Ian Shearer uses his chest to bring the ball under control.

He may be 30 and overweight but he's the only player I've got who can control a ball.

Brian Clough on John Robertson, 1983.

Turning
and Dribbling

Both these skills rely heavily on the sort of close control that can be learned only through many hours of practice. At one time every player could dribble like the gods, or so legend has it. The cumbersome boots and heavy ball of olden times suggest it was a specialized ability even then. However, it is true to say that until recently it was regarded as a dying art.

Opposite: Paul Gascoigne and John Barnes in training.

Below: Switzerland's Kubilay Türkyilmaz turns Gareth Southgate at Wembley.

The move away from street football, to organized matches on big pitches, resulted in fewer young players developing the sort of close control their predecessors had. So did the trend towards power football in which the capacity to run for 90 minutes was as prized as the ability to control a ball a few times during that period.

In recent years there has been a revival sparked by the introduction of foreign players like Georgiou Kinkladze and the emergence of talented young Englishmen like Steve McManaman. The spread of small-sided games and Dutch coaching techniques should ensure that the oldest art – originally players dribbled until tackled – continues to flourish to the delight of spectators everywhere.

Fundamentals

Before you can dribble you have to find the space to do so. Sometimes the ball will be received in enough space to take it at right angles, which is the best way of maintaining momentum. At other times you will have your back to a defender. The choice then is to play the ball backwards to a team-mate, or turn and beat your marker.

Your own ability, and your position on the pitch, will determine the answer. The nearer your own goal the greater the need to be cautious and pass. Further forward, a neat turn can take

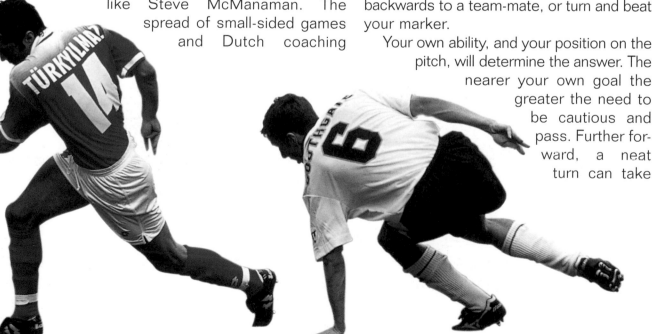

an opponent out of the game and create space to pass, shoot or dribble.

Initially you may need to screen the ball. This involves keeping your body between the ball and the opponent. You need to keep the ball in playing range, otherwise it will be obstruction. A variation on this theme is practised by defenders everywhere when preventing forwards reaching wayward passes before they go out for a goal kick or throw-in.

Once you have the ball under control, and the opponent behind or to your side, you need to turn him. A number of possible techniques follow. Experience, and your proficiency, will dictate which one you use in various situations. Personal practice will give you further variations.

Some of these techniques involve selling a dummy: making a move designed to fool the defender as to your real intention. The most basic of these is to pretend you are going to shoot or pass. Others feature body movement, such as dropping a shoulder or twisting a certain way, as if to indicate you are going to attempt to pass the player in that direction. Peter Beardsley's 'shimmy', for example, is all body and leg movement.

One alternative, though it rarely works at the highest level, is to fake a look, suggesting you are going to pass by looking, even indicating, that you will do so.

The key to all dummies is to be convincing.

Note: All turns are described with the right foot. For the left foot, reverse the procedure described. It is important to be good at both.

Turns For Receiving The Ball With Your Back To A Defender

Hook turn – inside
Both Kenny Dalglish and Franz Beckenbauer were particularly adept at this move, which is also known as 'cutting the ball'. Approach the ball slightly off-centre and stretch for it with the inside of the right foot, pivot on the left and turn past your left shoulder.

Hook turn – outside
A similar but easier to master move in which the ball is turned with the outside of the foot. This time receive the ball on the left side. Stretch for it with your right foot, step past the ball and then hook it to the right, pivoting on the left foot before turning around the defender's right shoulder.

Step over
A variation on the above turn which assumes you already have the ball under control. Shape up as though to play the ball to the left with the inside of the right foot, but step over it. Pivot on the right foot and take the ball away to the right with the left foot.

Turns When Under Pressure Running Crossfield With The Ball

Stop turn
Push the ball forward with the right foot, then step over and stop it with the right heel, or step on the ball with the right sole. Turn 180 degrees to the right and take the ball away with your left foot (or vice versa).

Gary McAllister of Scotland turns England's Paul Ince during Euro 96.

Manchester United's Ryan Giggs, a modern master of the ball.

Drag back

Shape up as if to play the ball in the direction you are going but kill it with the sole, drag the ball back and pivot through 180 degrees before moving off in the opposite direction.

Cruyff turn

A move made famous by Johan Cruyff, the great Dutch international. With the defender on your left, and the ball on your right foot, shape up as if to cross, pass or shoot to the left. As the defender commits himself to block the shot, place your foot over the ball and play it with the instep (if possible – the side of the foot or heel will usually do just as well) behind your left foot. You can then play the ball with your left foot or move in behind the defender. Easier than it sounds and very effective.

 INSIDE HOOK TURN: Pivoting on the left foot, the player turns round the defender's left shoulder as he plays the ball with his right foot.

TIPS FROM THE COACH

It takes hours of time and practice to learn good ball control, but the precious seconds it will gain you during a match will make that all worth while.

STEP OVER: The player feints to go right but puts his left foot over the ball. He then pushes off his left foot and takes the ball away to the left with his right foot.

CRUYFF TURN:
Having fooled the defender into thinking you are going to cross, you drag the ball behind your left foot with your right, gaining time and space.

OUTSIDE HOOK TURN:
Pivoting on the left foot the attacker turns round the defender's right shoulder by playing the ball with the outside of the right foot.

Dribbling

There is a difference between simply running with the ball and dribbling with it. When running with the ball you are often attacking space and you should aim to touch the ball as few times as possible. The fewer touches you take the quicker you will move, you will also have time between touches to look around and assess your options. You will soon find, however, that the space is closed down, in which case you should seek to attack an opponent.

When dribbling you are attacking an opponent at close range and should thus ensure the ball remains within your reach until you are past him. You should also restrain your speed. When you reach him, you will have to be controlled enough to beat him and slow enough to be able to accelerate.

Change of pace is one of the key weapons in a dribbler's armoury. The others are change of direction, close control – in which you may need to use every area of the foot – and a 'trick' or two. All the top dribblers have a trick, sometimes one unique to themselves, honed over hours of practice, and usually involving quick footwork and/or faking body movements.

The dribbler needs to be positive – hesitation plays into the hands of the defender. He should also be realistic – no one succeeds every time and most dribblers fail regularly, which is why dribbling should be avoided in defensive areas if at all possible.

Dribbling creates space by drawing opponents to one man and taking some of them out of the game. It also wins free-kicks. It should be remembered, however, that it is a means to an end, not an end in itself. If dribbling is to have any value, when the moment is right the ball should be released to a team-mate or a shot taken.

Techniques

There are many more variations on the following moves. Experiment by yourself, watch the top players to learn their 'tricks' and, if you are really keen, study the Coerver Method as formulated by the Dutch coach Wiel Coerver. But remember, it is better to learn a few tricks well than a lot of them badly. In a match you will need to get it right.

Matthews move

Named after Sir Stanley Matthews, the great English winger of the baggy-shorts generation. Lean to the left, dropping that shoulder as if you were going in that direction, and draw the ball to the left with the right foot. Then take it away to the right with the outside of the right foot, accelerating as you go.

The reverse 'Matthews' involves a double bluff. Having brought the ball left with the right foot, stop it with the left and drop the right shoulder, then swing back and take the ball away to the left with the inside of the right foot.

With both of these the key factor is the change of direction.

The locomotion

While running at the defender, shape to stop the ball with the sole of the foot, then drive it past him.

GREAT DRIBBLERS

JIMMY JOHNSTONE
(CELTIC & SCOTLAND)

GEORGE BEST
(MAN UTD & N. IRELAND)

STANLEY MATTHEWS
(STOKE, BLACKPOOL AND ENGLAND)

RYAN GIGGS
(MAN UTD & WALES)

Steve McManaman of Liverpool on the dribble. A thrilling sight – unless you are trying to stop him.

> "He's the only player I know who can dribble within a square metre."
>
> **Johan Cruyff, manager of Barcelona, on Romario.**

Stop-start

While running across the defender actually stop the ball with your right foot but then immediately drive it forward with the inside of the left. As with the previous move, it is the change of pace that makes this particular dribbling technique effective and wrong-foots the opposition.

The roll

As used by Davor Suker against Germany in Euro 96. While running towards the defender (in Suker's case the German goalkeeper), put the sole of your right foot on the ball and roll it to the left, thus steering the ball left, before driving on with the left foot.

Heading

Kevin Keegan, Robbie Fowler, Nick Barmby – all are well under six foot and all are good headers of the ball. You don't have to be a Duncan Ferguson or a Terry Butcher to be good in the air – it may help, but it is not everything. Trevor Brooking and Glenn Hoddle were both six-footers but no one remembers them for their heading ability. Brooking's 1980 FA Cup winner is recalled mainly because it was so rare.

Brooking was actually stooping for that goal, in the six-yard box, in the cup final. There can be no greater example of the way timing and positioning are as vital to heading as height. Those arts will be dealt with later, in the section on attacking football. This chapter is about technique.

Keegan, though 5 ft. 8 in. was a very good jumper. He realized early in his career that heading is not just about

Teddy Sheringham heads for
goal against Brazil during
the Umbro Cup competition.

using the head, it is about using the whole body.

There are two main types of header: the defensive and the attacking. Most defensive headers have one aim, to achieve distance and height to clear the danger. Attacking headers are about placement as much as power, and there is more variation with flick-ons, downward goal attempts and diving headers.

Techniques

For most headers aim to head the ball with the centre of the forehead while keeping the eyes open until the moment of impact (when they will briefly close involuntarily). Young players often find this difficult and they should be taught with great care at first. If they come to associate heading with pain, they will become poor headers.

Headed properly, the ball will not hurt. Jack Charlton always tells young players to wet a spot on their forehead between the eyes (but above the eyebrows) and wave their hand in front of it. The spot should go cold – that is where to head the ball. Heading with the bridge of the nose will obviously hurt, and the ball won't go far. Heading with the top of the head will often hurt, and the ball could go anywhere.

The guiding principle is to attack the ball, not to let the ball attack you. Whether heading from a standing or jumping position the back should arch and the neck muscles tense before impact. The head should be pulled back. As you thrust the head forward to head the ball, the arms should go back to provide added leverage. For height, head the bottom half of the ball.

Direction is determined by the position of the head, so you should twist the body to aim, pivoting on the hips. At contact the upper body should be almost at right angles. Forwards will be looking to head down and away from the goalkeeper, normally towards a corner of the goal. Defenders will be seeking to head the ball upfield and towards the flanks where the ball is less likely to be volleyed straight back.

Directing a flick-on, glance or deflection is slightly different and was dealt with on page 19, under Head pass.

Showing bravery and timing, Alex McLeish rises high above John Fashanu, Stuart Pearce and Des Walker during an England–Scotland game.

Patrick Kluivert attempts a
brave diving header during
Holland's draw with Scotland
in Euro 96.

Heading from a jumping position

Where possible, head from a standing position; it provides better balance. Jumping off one leg, on the run, gives more height to the jump; jumping off two, from a standing start, more accuracy because of the better balance.

The techniques are slightly different. Jumping off both feet, your lower legs should be pulled up behind the knees then whipped forward at the same time as the head. Jumping off one foot, the take-off leg goes back, the other leg 'climbs' in order to be pushed down to provide extra height. This may sound complicated, but the action largely happens naturally.

In both cases as the head goes forward the arms go back and down to provide added leverage (take care with elbows).

Diving headers

All headers require timing and courage but none as much as the diving header. This skill often involves putting your head among flying boots but, when well executed, is very hard to prevent. It can carry a measure of surprise and is sometimes the only way of reaching a ball.

Diving headers can be glanced or met full on – which gives maximum power because your body weight will be behind the shot. Again you should aim to meet the ball with the forehead.

3 When you are in position above the ball, make contact with it using the middle of your forehead.

2 Arch your back and thrust your body forwards to ensure there is power in the shot when you make contact with the ball.

1 Watch the ball as you rise to meet it, pushing off from the ground with both legs.

Tackling

When an American gridiron football team loses possession they stop the play, bring off the forwards and bring on the defenders. There used to be association footballers who effectively did much the same, departing the game in spirit, if not in body, whenever possession was lost. Not any more. Now, with a few rare exceptions, everyone defends and everyone, including the goalkeeper, needs to tackle.

Tackling is an art, a destructive one but an art none the less. Good tackles can transform defence into attack within seconds. Bad tackles can cost a match.

Defending in pairs and as a unit is dealt with later in this book. This chapter is devoted to individual contests.

How you defend will depend on whether your team uses the zonal or man-marking system of defence. These will also be dealt with later, but, for the purposes of this chapter, we will assume that, as the opposition move towards you, you are either marking an opponent or being attacked by one. Tackling is mostly about attitude.

Approach

There are three options open to a defender as the attack enters his area: Intercept, make a 50–50 tackle, or jockey.

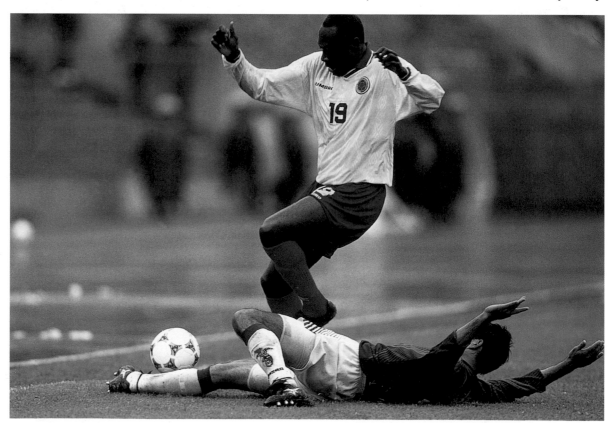

A Bolivian boot halts the run of Freddy Rincon of Colombia.

Intercept

The best way to tackle an opponent is to prevent the ball reaching him. It means you take possession unchallenged and remove an opponent from the play. Experience in reading the game will tell you when this is possible. Be aware that failure carries a high penalty, as your man will be left unmarked and in possession while you will be badly positioned.

50-50 tackle

If interception is impossible or too risky the next choice is to tackle your opponent before he can get the ball under control. This means tackling as he receives possession. The key is to make the challenge not a 50–50 one, where you both theoretically have an equal chance, but a 60–40 or 70–30. This is achieved by getting to the ball first, through a combination of experience and determination. You can then win the ball with a head-on tackle (see below) or simply 'toe' the ball away. Remember that tackling from behind has now been outlawed, and if you try and tackle through a player's legs you are risking dismissal.

Jockey

He has either got there first, or is already in possession and dribbling towards you. Different problems, same ambition – to delay him and force him to do what you want him to do.

In the first case the aim is to prevent him turning. Stay within three or four feet and watch the ball, not his body. The time to tackle is when he attempts to turn; he is likely to be off-balance and you have a sight of the ball. Use a 'confronting' block tackle, or simply a 'toe'. Remember, be patient, the onus is on him to do something, and defenders will be flooding back in support (you hope).

Dealing with the dribbler also requires patience and concentration. Watch the ball, not the man, so you will not be conned by feints. Maybe attempt a feint yourself to change the emphasis – though be careful not to become off-balance.

You should be standing slightly side-on, so you are already half-turned if he pushes

the ball past you; it also makes it less likely you will be embarrassed by a 'nutmeg' – when the ball is played through your legs.

Which way you turn will depend on whether you want to show him 'down the line' or 'inside'. This is usually determined by the support you have, if any, and the strengths of your team. Some prefer to force players wide, some try to bring them inside where there is usually less space. If you can, force your opponent onto his bad foot; i.e. make a right-footed player play with his left foot – always look to see which your opponent favours early in a game.

If possible, stay on your feet. You can lose valuable seconds recovering from a tackle that leaves you on the ground.

Paul Gascoigne attempts to tackle Stewart McKimmie during Euro 96's Anglo-Scottish encounter.

Techniques
Block tackle 1

There are two tackles known as the block tackle. This one is used when directly confronting an opponent and requires strength, timing and, in young players, confidence.

Only the foot makes contact, but the whole body makes the tackle. Approach the ball as if making a side-on pass and meet it solidly with the side of the foot. The body should be tensed with the main leverage coming from the groin. Come in low from a crouching position, head forward. Made well, this tackle should move the ball behind the attacker.

Young players are sometimes nervous about the physical nature of this tackle. It can hurt, but only if you do it half-heartedly, then you will be knocked out of the way by the opponent. The firmer your tackle, the less likely you are to be hurt. But make sure you play the ball and not the man.

Block tackle 2

This version is made as the forward attempts to shoot, cross or pass. As he prepares to kick, get one or both legs into the likely path of the ball. Care should be taken on two counts. Be sure he is not selling you a dummy, as you will be left out of position, and try to get fully in the way or you could cause an unfortunate deflection.

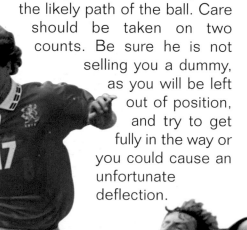

Stewart McKimmie pushes the ball away from Jordi Cruyff with a slide tackle.

Side tackle

As referred to in 50–50 tackle on the previous page. As you and the forward move towards the ball, try and get your foot around it first and steer it away with the inside of the foot.

Slide tackle

It looks good and is fun on a wet, muddy surface, but the slide tackle is the tackle of last resort. This is because it looks horrible when it goes wrong – and can lead to a booking or worse – and leaves the defender on the floor. If you have to do it, try and ensure the ball is forced out of play.

Timing and agility are the key factors. While running alongside your opponent, take off on the inner foot and swing the outer foot around your body as you fall feet first. The outer foot should either push the ball away or hook itself round the ball. Keep the tackle low to avoid tripping the opponent.

Shoulder charge

This is no longer a legal challenge on the goalkeeper but, within limits, is still acceptable elsewhere on the pitch although not as common as it used to be. You need to be alongside your opponent and can only use the shoulder – not the elbow or arms. The ball needs to be within playing distance.

To make the challenge, crouch slightly then force yourself into your opponent using all your body weight and pushing up off one leg. With the other leg try and play the ball across your opponent while he is unbalanced.

Toe

Some players are regarded as being great 'toe-rs'. Chris Perry, of Wimbledon, is one. They have this ability to 'get a toe in' and nudge the ball away from a forward just as he believes he has beaten the defender. This is often more effective than a full-blooded tackle because it leaves the defender upright. Experience, timing and agility are the key factors.

RISKY MOVES

1 **SHOULDER CHARGE:**
Push into your opponent with the shoulder, having 'pushed up' from the legs for power.

TIPS FROM THE COACH

When attempting any tackle, always play the ball, not the man.

•

In a shoulder challenge, make contact only with the other player's shoulder, otherwise you may be penalized.

1 **SLIDE TACKLE:**
The tackle of last resort. Make sure you play the ball, not your opponent's legs.

Goalkeeping

Goalkeeping used to be a neglected aspect of football. The least athletic boy was placed in goal and little thought was given to development of the keeper's skills at a higher level. This was foolish, because poor goalkeepers can lose a game while the assurance of good goalkeepers brings better performances from the players around them.

In the last 20 years this importance has been increasingly recognized. Transfer fees have risen and a growing number of professional clubs employ specialist goalkeeper coaches.

The nature of goalkeeping has also changed. Bruce Grobbelaar was often criticized for his penchant for leaving his goal area, but the way he came for the ball within it made every English goalkeeper rethink his game. Goalkeepers are now prepared to come a dozen yards or more to collect crosses, and wingers have had to adapt their own approach accordingly.

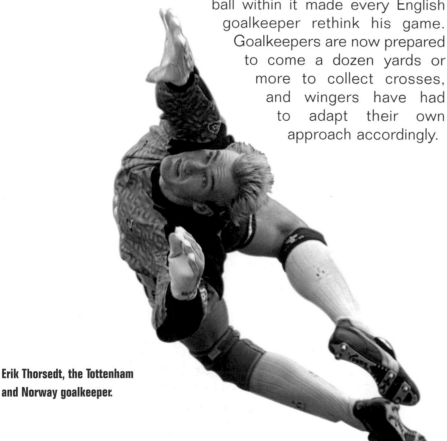

Erik Thorsedt, the Tottenham and Norway goalkeeper.

Fundamentals

The physical attributes required of a goalkeeper are obvious: agility, sharp reflexes, good hands and, ideally, both speed of movement and a commanding build. Smaller players can compensate to an extent with timing and a command of angles but height and a certain amount of bulk make goalkeeping easier.

But the physical side is only one aspect of being a good No.1. More than any other position, goalkeeping requires a combination of technical skill and mental aptitude. It is an exposed role; mistakes usually cost a goal, and bad ones are recalled for years afterwards. David Seaman was outstanding in Arsenal's 1995 European Cup-Winners' Cup run, and without his saves in open play in Auxerre and the penalty shoot-out in Sampdoria they would never have made the final. Once there he kept them in the game with a series of saves. And what is he remembered for? Being beaten by Real Zaragoza's Nayim from 50 yards, a goal that owed as much to luck and Nayim's gambler's instinct as goalkeeping error.

Goalkeepers in good sides have to be able to retain concentration during long periods without action. The change in the back-pass law means that many more have to act as sweeper as well as goalkeeper – goalkeeper is no longer a hiding place for a footballer who cannot kick.

Along with concentration and mental strength, there is one other quality a goalkeeper must have in abundance – courage. That does not just mean physical bravery, but also the courage of conviction, the courage to make and accept responsibility for decisions, such as claiming crosses.

Techniques

A few basic principles can be applied to any save -

- Be ready.
- Expect a shot or cross at all times and stay well-balanced, on the balls of your feet rather than on your heels.
- Watch the ball and get behind the line of its flight whenever possible.
- Catch it if you can. Take the ball with your hands in a 'W' shape with the finger and arm muscles relaxed (as with an outfield player making a 'soft' trap). Secure the ball within the shell of your body by pulling it into the stomach as soon as you can.
- If you have to parry or deflect the ball, direct it out to the side in case forwards are following up and get to your feet quickly.
- Be in constant communication with your defenders. You have a better view of the play than any of them, so tell them when players are being left unmarked.
- If you want the ball, call for it quickly and clearly. If you don't, ensure the defender knows it is his responsibility.
- Finally, never panic. It is contagious and defenders are particularly susceptible to catching it from goalkeepers.

Saves without Diving

For a ball on the ground

There are two ways of making this save, forwards or sideways. In both the aim is to get the body behind the ball and guide it right into the stomach region.

Forwards: With palms down the goalkeeper moves towards the ball and scoops it up. He can go down on his knees first or, more commonly, stoop with his legs close together.

Sideways: A more popular method, similar to the 'long barrier' in cricket. The goalkeeper goes down on one knee, ensuring the heel of the upright foot is just behind the knee of the sideways one. The ball is again scooped up with palms down.

For a ball at ankle to waist height

Again, two methods: Standing and falling.

Standing: Bend the knees sideways and waist forward to take the ball, palms down, at a comfortable height.

Falling: A popular method with continental 'keepers – the ball is taken in the stomach area by diving towards it; the arms fold in behind the ball to secure it.

For a ball at chest or head height

There comes a point when it is more comfortable to take the ball with the palms up. This is usually when the ball has risen to chest height. Stand up straight and catch the ball in front of the body, allowing yourself space to 'give' with the ball. You may need to jump a bit to make the height comfortable.

For a ball above head height

Take the ball in front of you, allowing for 'give' and pull it down into the chest area, wrapping your elbows around it.

David Seaman of Arsenal showing good skills as he dives to save – his eyes fixed firmly on the flight of the ball.

Diving Saves

If you have to dive for the ball, do not hesitate. If you do, it will be too late. If you land properly, it should not hurt unduly – nor should you spill the ball. Always brace yourself for the landing, keeping the arms relaxed to absorb the impact.

For a ball on the ground

The hardest save. How you make it will depend on how close the ball is to your body. If it is near, whip your legs from under you and fall onto the ball. For slightly further away, collapse only the nearest leg. If the ball is quite distant, dive with both feet extended. Always try and get hands to the ball with the body following behind.

For a ball in the air

Take off from the leg nearest the ball, twisting as you fall to gather the ball under your body. Try and take the ball in front of you, allowing you to absorb the power of the shot.

Other Saves

When to parry or deflect

When the shot is too strong to hold, or too distant to catch, parry or deflect it. Use two hands whenever possible and direct the ball away from the goal. The exception is where there is no attacker near by; then you should parry the ball down in front of you to take the sting out of the shot.

Taking crosses

Make the decision early and stick to it, but time your run as late as possible. This will enable you to assess the flight of the ball, the best place to meet it, and provide maximum height and momentum from a one-footed jump. Call for the ball. Time your jump to meet the ball at the top of the jump.

Punching

If you cannot guarantee safely catching a cross, punch it. Use two hands if possible and jab at the ball, hitting the bottom half. Aim to punch the ball high and far towards the sidelines. One-handed punches have less power and accuracy, but can reach higher crosses.

Tipping the ball over the bar

Too high to catch? Too risky to punch? Tip it. Use the open palm and, one-handed for greater height, deflect the ball over the bar. This can also be used for helping on crosses which are too high to punch.

Narrowing the angle

Even Billy 'Fatty' Foulke, the legendary 22-stone Chelsea goalkeeper, could not fill the entire goal frame. Neither will you but, if you narrow the angle, you can look as if you have. Peter Shilton was expert at 'making himself big' this way. He was only 14 stone but, to many attackers, he filled the goal.

Judging angles is as crucial to a goalkeeper as a snooker player and, unlike the latter, a goalkeeper has to do it blind, with his back to goal.

When you guard your goal, or advance on a forward, try to imagine two lines extending from the ball to each post. You should be in a position where you can touch either of these lines.

There is one important proviso: if you go too far out you will be vulnerable to the chip. How far you go out is a compromise between narrowing the angle and being able to get back and save a chip.

One-on-one

Narrowing the angle is most important when you find yourself in a one-on-one situation. So is staying on your feet. Make the forward take the decision. If he decides to shoot, try and get close enough to block the ball. If he tries to go round you, force him as wide as you can before spreading yourself and attacking the ball with your hands. Be careful, this is where penalties are conceded.

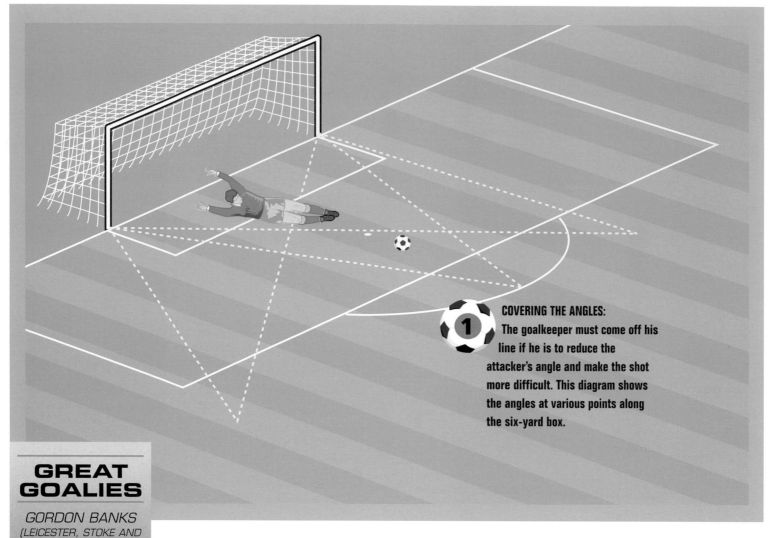

COVERING THE ANGLES:
The goalkeeper must come off his line if he is to reduce the attacker's angle and make the shot more difficult. This diagram shows the angles at various points along the six-yard box.

GREAT GOALIES

GORDON BANKS
(LEICESTER, STOKE AND ENGLAND)

NEVILLE SOUTHALL
(EVERTON AND WALES)

PAT JENNINGS
(TOTTENHAM, ARSENAL AND N. IRELAND)

DINO ZOFF
(JUVENTUS AND ITALY)

Opposite: Peter Schmeichel gathers a cross for Manchester United against Blackburn Rovers.

Distribution

Peter Schmeichel is a fine example of how a goalkeeper can also be a playmaker. His throw-outs frequently release Manchester United attacks, especially when Andrei Kanchelskis was on the wing.

Schmeichel delivers the ball like a bowler in cricket, combining distance and accuracy. For shorter passes, especially on hard or artificial surfaces, bowl underarm; this way the ball is received on the ground and is easier to control.

Bear in mind that, while a quick throw can start a counter-attack, executing it too early can cost a goal. Make the save first and don't look around until the ball has been secured. On no account throw to the side

from which the ball has been received.

Kicking, on the drop volley or half-volley, gets greater distance but at the sacrifice of accuracy.

With goalkeepers now banned from picking up backpasses, fly-kicking has become an important element of goalkeeping. This has led to some hilarious goals, even at top level, with the ball being poorly controlled and goalkeepers dispossessed, or kicked at a forward and rebounding into goal.

If you can, stop the ball and pass it to a team-mate, but the priority is to get rid of it safely. Not only is a goalkeeper rarely as adept with the ball as an outfielder, but he is also in the position of greatest risk.

> **" Probably the only play-making goalkeeper in the country. "**
>
> **Alan Hodgkinson, Manchester United's goalkeeping coach, on Peter Schmeichel.**

Part II:
Developing Tactics

Four-four-two, catenaccio, split-strikers, wing-backs... Football, like most occupations, has spawned its own lexicon, and no area is more riddled with it than tactics. To some this is all rubbish – the game is about players and good players will beat bad ones. To others, this is a Luddite philosophy. Darren Anderton, talking about life at Tottenham in Ossie Ardiles' reign, once told me 'the football was enjoyable but Ossie used to say "you are good players, go out and play". The 11 best players in the world are not going to make a team, it depends how they gel together.' Systems do not make a team but neither do players. Good players, well organized, make a good team.

These days most good sides are based on defence and built around a strong spine running from the goalkeeper to the leader of the attack. How they are arranged will depend on the preference of the coach and the individual strengths of the players. Some coaches, such as the former Italian coach Arrigio Sacchi, decide upon a system then find players to fit. Less well-resourced coaches devise a system to fit their players, while others will vary it according to circumstances.

Some teams, especially at higher levels, or against better teams, adapt their system to counter the opposition. Outside factors, such as the climate (high temperatures often lead to a slower match, strong winds to a disjointed one) and the pitch (wide ones favour wing play, frozen ones help forwards), can also affect the nature of the game.

The emphasis in some teams is on 'set-plays'. For many years the Football Association officially backed the idea of 'direct play', which concentrates on moving the ball forward quickly and trying to score from subsequent corners, free-kicks, etc. At its worst, this style was little more than a refined version of the schoolyard kick-and-rush.

While many goals are scored from such set-pieces, and teams need to be prepared for them, a personal belief is that this only works up to a certain level. As players get better and defences more organized, greater subtlety is required to break them down. The Republic of Ireland, under Jack Charlton, gained a measure of

Togetherness – Brazil enjoy that winning feeling after winning the 1994 World Cup.

success with an adaptation of such tactics but rarely beat the best teams.

A range of tempo and technique, as practised by the Brazilians, is more penetrating and much more attractive to watch. By mixing up long and short passing, interspersing periods of passing with dribbles or making shots, opponents are kept guessing and forced to think.

Whatever system a team uses, how they play will depend on attitude as much as formation; for example, 3-5-2 can be ultra-defensive or very attacking. Selfishness, fear, indiscipline and stupidity can undo the best systems. To that extent, football is all about players.

Formations

Early football teams were little more than a collection of players running after the ball. Formations appeared in the second half of the 19th century with the movement towards the standardization of rules.

In England, where the game was all about dribbling, this initially meant a goalkeeper, one back, one half-back and eight dribbling forwards. This changed after the introduction of the FA Cup in 1872 which, during its first 15 years, featured Scottish clubs, such as Rangers and Queen's Park, who placed a greater emphasis on passing. Thus, by the time the Football League was formed in 1888, clubs had begun to adopt the 2-3-5 (two backs, three half-backs, five forwards) formation which persisted until the change in the offside law nearly 40 years later.

When that happened, in 1925, the immediate result was a massive increase in goals as forwards enjoyed their new freedom (the rule reduced the number of defenders required between a forward and the goal from three to the present-day two). The long-term result was a move to three defenders. Herbert Chapman, the legendary manager of Huddersfield and Arsenal, is widely credited with the ploy, which he developed to form the WM formation, a 3-4-3 or 3-3-4 in modern-day terms.

While there were variations on this formation, notably Don Revie playing as a deep-lying centre-forward, more than 30 years passed before there were further changes. Then, inspired by the success of Hungary and Real Madrid, coaches like Ron Greenwood and Dick Graham began to experiment with sweepers and more fluid formations. However, the most significant development for the domestic game was Alf Ramsey's wingless 4-4-2, which won the World Cup for England in 1966.

This formation influenced the English game for decades. Meanwhile, Continental sides were moving in different directions. Defensive developments were highlighted at Internazionale of Milan in Italy by Helenio Herrera's introduction of catenaccio, with two markers and a sweeper. This was contrasted a decade later by the Dutch philosophy of 'total football', based on the talents of Ajax's Johan Cruyff and positional flexibility. Two decades later Ajax of Amsterdam again led the way, this time with an updated version, 1-3-3-3, with which they won the European Cup.

More successful than any were the

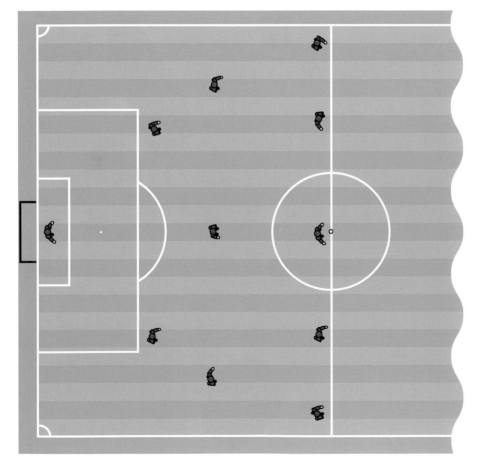

Football Victorian style: the very attacking and very vulnerable 2-3-5 formation.

Germans, who were among the first to develop the sweeper's role by introducing an element of creativity and attacking play to his game. Helmut Schön was the architect with Franz Beckenbauer the player who implemented his theory. This practice has continued to the present day with Matthias Sammer being the latest to adopt Beckenbauer's mantle.

English clubs remained rooted in 4-4-2 for so long that, in the early 1990s, a football magazine was named after it. Ironically, this was just as English clubs were beginning to adopt Continental ideas and European ones, like Milan, were moving to 4-4-2, now rechristened 'the pressing game'.

Euro '96 saw the most innovative England side yet. Several English teams, including Chelsea, Aston Villa and Liverpool, had adopted the Continental 3-5-2 formation but adapted it to English players. They fielded three central defenders at the back and attacking full-backs as the flank players in the midfield. This is similar to the German formation that won Euro 96, except there was no English equivalent of Matthias Sammer, the archetypal European sweeper, who would frequently step into midfield to support the attack.

Under Terry Venables England had a back three of one central defender (Tony Adams) and two full-backs (Gary Neville and Stuart Pearce). One of the midfielders (Paul Ince or Gareth Southgate) was deputed to drop back into defence when necessary. The flank players were wingers (Darren Anderton and Steve McManaman). Newcastle United adopted a similar formation at times in the subsequent domestic season.

One variation was against the Dutch when England played the 'Christmas Tree': a conventional back four, three midfielders, two 'inside-forwards' and Alan Shearer as a lone central striker. This had been heavily criticized for not creating chances, but England went out and scored four.

At other times Venables played with split, rather than twin, strikers. This meant Shearer playing as the focal point of the attack and Teddy Sheringham taking up a slightly deeper position to link him with

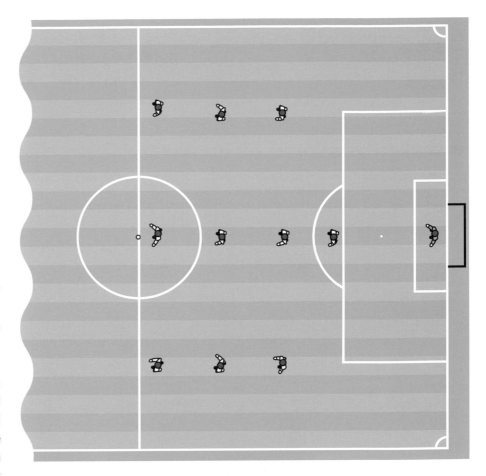

Above: **The fluid Ajax 1-3-3-3 system.**

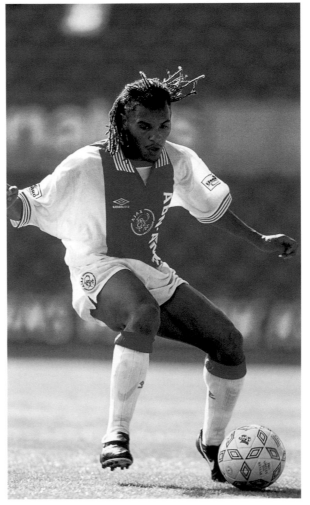

Left: **Nordin Wooter of Ajax.**

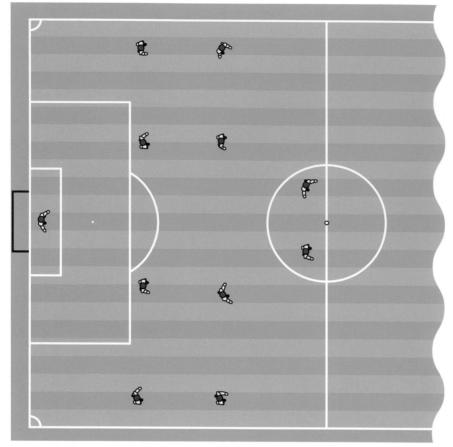

Above: Solid and successful, 4-4-2 has worked for England in 1966 and Milan in the 1990s.

Below: Playing the numbers game – 3-5-2 gives strength in midfield.

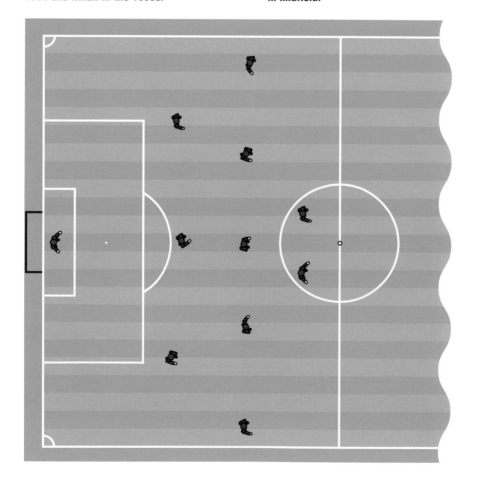

midfield rather than playing alongside him.

Systems continue to evolve as coaches search for ways to outwit increasingly organized defences. When a country such as Liechtenstein can hold the Republic of Ireland to a draw the effectiveness of well-planned defending, and the need for clever attacking to defeat it, is obvious.

The Basic Systems:
Pros and Cons

4-4-2

At its simplest, with the midfield four in a horizontal line, this is easy to understand and organize and is thus a good system for young players. The two wide midfield players need to be athletic and good crossers because they will be providing both attacking width and defensive cover. The forwards need to use the space available on the flanks. The defence is a conventional back four.

The midfield can be a diamond pattern with one playing anchor in front of the defence and another pushing forward to support the front two. This requires greater tactical awareness. At top level, defenders need the flexibility to step into midfield if they find they are confronted by only one striker. Otherwise their team will be outnumbered in midfield.

3-5-2

This provides numbers in midfield and a solid defensive core. Its disadvantage is that it can be exposed defensively on the flanks if the wide players are attacking by nature (as with David Ginola at Newcastle). Wide players need to be very fit.

4-5-1

A demanding role for the sole striker, who has to find space when outnumbered to receive the ball, then hold it up while waiting for support. It provides numbers in midfield but some of them need to be ready to push forward at the slightest opportunity.

4-3-3

Sometimes thought to be a traditional Scottish formation with the third forward being a winger; or, as played by Ajax, with two wingers and a central striker and one of the central defenders dropping back to be a sweeper. Players need to be flexible if they are not to be outnumbered in midfield.

Opposite: Wing-backs in opposition – Sergi of Spain and England's Gary Neville.

Defending

In the modern game, everyone defends. As soon as the ball is lost a team should be working to disrupt the opposition and get it back. This can mean the centre-forward harrying defenders to prevent them playing an accurate pass (as Ian Rush did so well for Liverpool), or the winger marking the full-back to prevent the goalkeeper finding him with a quick throw.

The next barrier is the midfield which, as will be shown in the next chapter, can operate in a variety of ways to break up attacks.

Eventually though, however good the front and midfield players are, the defence will be called upon.

There are two main ways of defending, zonal and man-to-man. Both have their

Five at the back – in this scheme the full-backs have flexible roles.

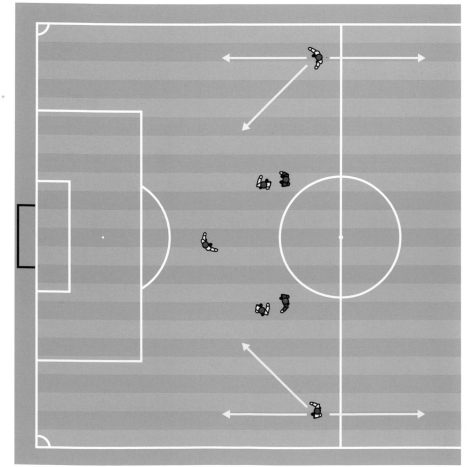

strengths and weaknesses and sometimes a combination of the two is used in an attempt to counter these. Zonal marking is generally preferred by English clubs, man-to-man by many Continental sides. The contrast between the two systems is commonly seen when English clubs come up against their European counterparts.

Zonal

This can be played with a back three, four or five, but is easier with four. Each defender is responsible for an area and picks up attackers as they enter it. Obviously this has to be flexible, otherwise one defender could end up marking two players while his partner watches.

Communication between defenders is vital, because as forwards move across the defence they need to be 'passed on' from one defender to another. This procedure will often be dropped near to goal, or when an attack is sustained with many forwards involved. In these cases, players stick with their man until it is either convenient to swap or danger elsewhere forces them to mark another forward.

One advantage of the zonal system is that usually it gives the defence a spare man to provide cover. When the opposition have the ball he should try to cover his colleagues. When his own team have it, he should provide an outlet for a pass.

If a back four are being attacked on one flank, the full-back on the other should be

Right: **A zonal-marking system in action – each defender is ready to cover a team mate.**

looking to cover the central defenders. His own man will be far enough from the danger for him to recover should the ball be switched. The exception to this is when the attack is near goal, then he should be aiming to pick up his man, unless there is an unmarked forward in a more dangerous position.

In a zonal system, defenders are able to conserve energy as a forward is passed from one to another and they are able to stay within areas where they are comfortable. Big blocking players should not need to be pulled out to the wings, and small full-backs should not find themselves dealing with high crosses in the six-yard box.

Problems can occur when there is a shortage of players to mark. Central defenders are often unwilling to step into midfield to find their man and make up the numbers. Full-backs are usually more prepared to push forward, but there is a danger of leaving exploitable gaps if they do so without care.

Defenders should also be wary of allowing forwards to get between them – a forward is still a threat even when he is outnumbered.

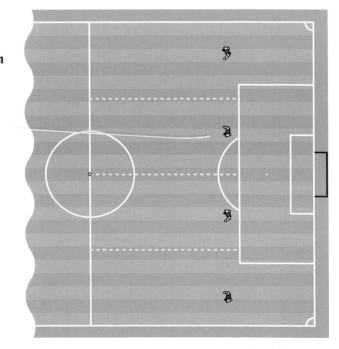

Right: **Basic areas for a zonal-marking system. Man-marking takes over in the penalty area.**

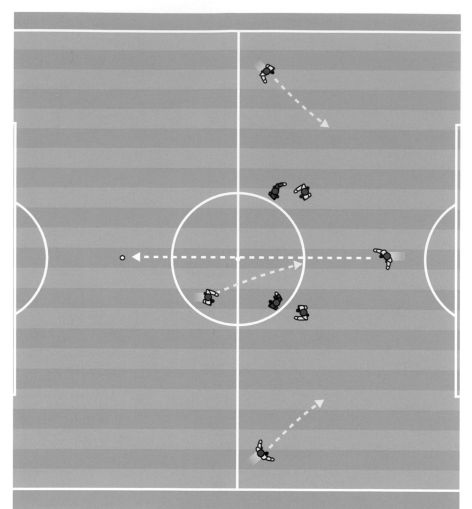

Above: **As a sweeper moves forwards, a midfielder or the full-backs should be prepared to cover.**

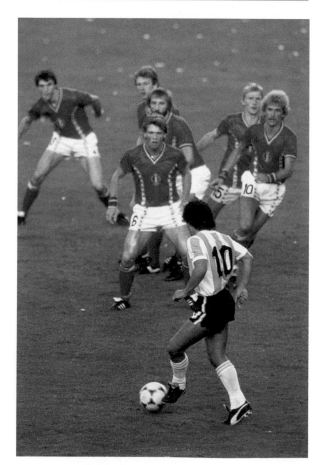

Right: **Maradona finds Belgium taking the principle of defensive cover to extremes.**

Man-to-man

Usually played with a sweeper, this system makes greater demands on concentration but less on 'reading' the game. Each defender is assigned a forward to mark and he sticks with him regardless of other action. Obviously if a goal threatens he may have to challenge another player, but in the usual course of events he will follow his forward around the pitch.

The marker needs to be as fit as his opponent and equally adept in the centre and on the flanks. He should always be close enough to challenge his opponent just as he receives the ball – which is when he is most vulnerable.

One problem with this system from a team perspective is that it is hard to cover a colleague who is being overwhelmed by his opponent.

Combined Defending

Collective man-to-man marking is still a rarity in the English game, but the practice of individual man-marking complementing a zonal system is becoming more common. Players such as Matt Le Tissier and Steve McManaman encounter it on a regular basis as teams assign one defender to follow them regardless of the rest of the game. Sometimes this works, often it does not. Man-marking is a precise skill and there are few English players (Martin Keown is one) possessed of the single-mindedness and all-round capability to do it.

Marking

The technique of marking is the same for zonal or man-to-man defences. The defender should be close to his opponent, ideally close enough to prevent him from turning upon receipt of the ball but not so close that it is easy to play the ball in behind him.

He should also be 'goalside', between the forward and the goal; in a position to see the ball and the forward simultaneously; and in a position, such as half-turned, from which he can move quickly if the ball is played past him for the attacker to run on to.

When the ball is played towards his man,

he should aim to intercept it or challenge as it arrives. If the odds are against this, he should not dive in, because over-committing will lead to being turned or committing a foul.

Keeping 'goalside' is most important when an attack is near to goal. The defender should operate within an imaginary triangle whose points are the goal, the ball, and the man he is marking. This gives him every chance of being first to a cross played in front of his man – balls played behind him are far less dangerous.

Watch the man, not just the ball.

Sweeper

The sweeper literally 'sweeps up' behind his team-mates, covering them in case a forward breaks free, or a ball is played over the top or into channels.

The sweeper needs to have a good understanding of the game and be more comfortable on the ball than most defenders. On the Continent, where he is also called a libero, he is also seen as a supplementary forward, carrying the ball into midfield whenever the opportunity arises and thus disrupting the opposition's marking scheme.

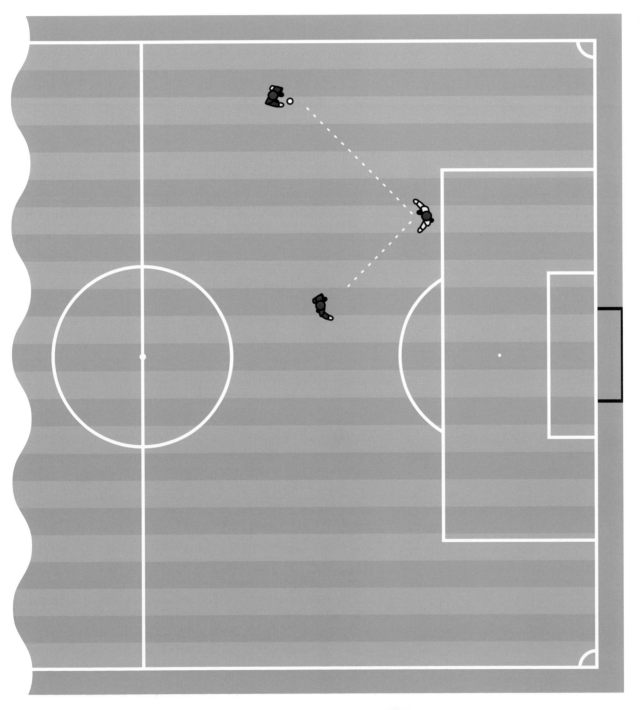

The defender is keeping the ball and 'his man' within sight. If the ball is played towards 'his man', he is well placed to intercept.

One defender shows the attacker outside while the other moves across to cover.

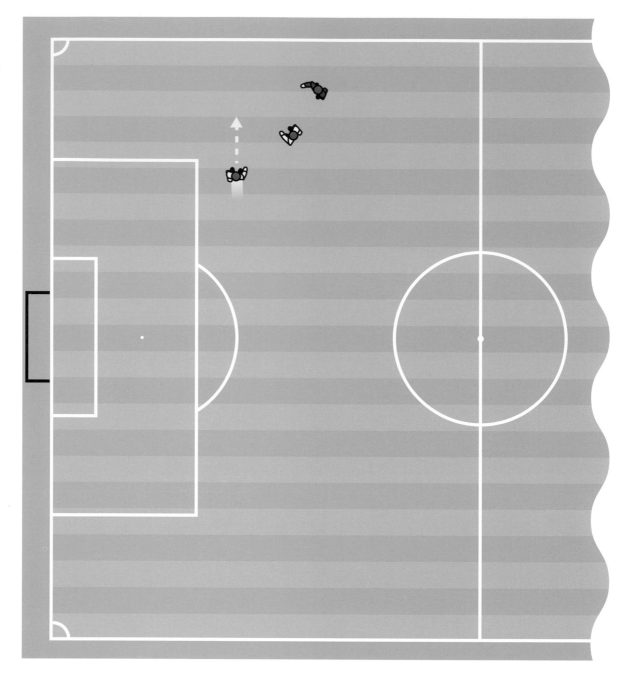

Below: Showing an attacker inside.

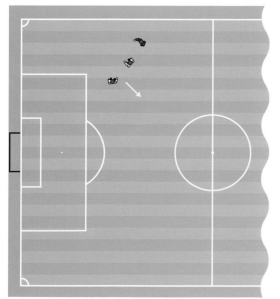

The sweeper's position is determined by that of the ball. He should be in position to react to danger and, if a team-mate is engaged in tackling or jockeying a forward, he should be close enough to provide assistance. If the markers are occupied, he goes to the man on the ball.

'Inside' and 'Outside'

When Terry Venables became coach of Barcelona he inherited a team used to pushing opponents outside, to the flanks. He got them to push opponents inside, to the centre. The Spanish defenders were dubious at first but early success convinced them.

Both methods have their advantages, and which one to use depends on the strengths of both your team and the opposition. A team with a strong-tackling, well-staffed centre, both midfield and defence, will seek to push players inside, especially if their opponents have good crossers and headers of the ball.

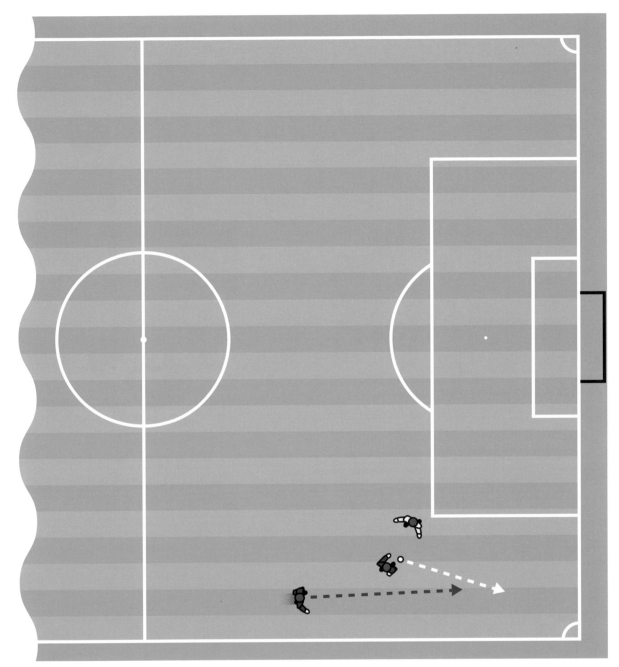

The overlapping full-back can be very effective.

Other teams prefer to push players outside, especially if that forces them onto the wrong foot. Such teams might have tall centre-halves and quick full-backs.

Deep – or pushed up?

As well as changing Barcelona's method of shepherding forwards, Terry Venables also changed the defence's basic position. This had been used to sitting deep and drawing attacks onto them. He made them push up, like most English defences do, and squeeze the space in midfield.

As well as restricting the opposition's space, pushing up means that attacks can be confronted further away from the

danger area. Opponents will often resort to playing long balls over the top which can usually be picked up or cleared by the goalkeeper. It also makes the offside trap easier to play.

Sitting deep tends to put pressure on defences because it enables the opposing team to get much closer to goal. On the plus side it enables teams to retain their compactness, benefiting those sides whose game is based on the frequent interchange of short passes. Opponents can also be vulnerable to swift counter-attacks, especially if they have committed too many men forward. It also benefits teams who are strong in the air defensively.

Defender 1 is beaten but quickly makes a recovery run behind defender 2, who has delayed the forward. He will now have to beat defender 1 again.

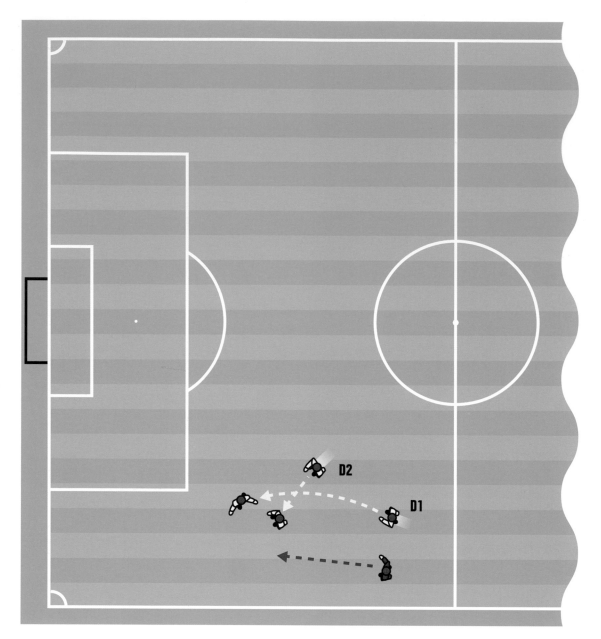

Support Play

One of the chief requirements of any defence is to prevent attackers creating a one-on-one position. If a defender knows he has a team-mate behind him, he will immediately feel much more secure and his opponent less ambitious. The attack is thus likely to be delayed before a tackle is made.

The tackler and the supporting player should work as a partnership. Their stance will depend on team tactics and field positions. When the attack is down the centre of the field the defence will usually try and push the forward away from goal. When it is in a wide position, their movement depends on whether they wish to push the opponent inside or outside.

If the defence is seeking to push the player outside, the first defender will stand slightly across the forward, barring his route inside and inviting him to go the other way. His stance should be half-turned, enabling him to run with the forward should he accept. Meanwhile the supporting defender should have taken up a position about two yards behind his team-mate and on the side to which the forward is being encouraged to go. He should shout to his team-mate to indicate his position. The first defender will then try to steer the forward into the path of the second. If the action occurs on the flanks, the defenders will try and shepherd the forward into touch.

If the aim is to show the forward inside, the first defender will bar the direct route and allow the player to run across him. Again, he is half-turned to run in that direction. The second defender should stand in a similar position slightly deeper and further across the field.

The second defender should beware of getting too close to the first, because he may find himself beaten in the same movement the forward uses to go past his team-mate. Stand further back for quick players, closer in for skilled dribblers. Gerry Armstrong's skip between two Spanish defenders before creating Billy Hamilton's goal in Northern Ireland's famous 1982 World Cup is a classic example of two defenders being beaten in one movement.

There are times when a defender has to be left to fend for himself. This is usually when he is being attacked down the wing and the defence is short of numbers in the centre. In that case the other defenders should hold the centre.

Marking Space

Sometimes the last man is confronted by a player attacking, unhindered by defenders, while he marks a team-mate lurking with intent in the centre. In this position the last defender has to mark space.

He moves towards the man on the ball with a view to preventing him shooting, while also attempting to hold a position that gives him a chance of intercepting a pass. Obviously this is pretty difficult, but it is amazing how often a forward, presented with two difficult options, will fail to manage either.

Recovery Runs

If a defender is beaten, or caught out of position, his first thought should be to make a recovery run. This is made with the intention of meeting or blocking the man on the ball, of taking up a supporting position behind the team-mate challenging the man on the ball, or of picking up an unmarked opponent or unguarded space.

Every player should look to be making a recovery run as soon as possession is lost. The quicker a team regains its 'shape' the more effectively it can thwart an attack.

Martin Keown shadows Paul Goddard.

Germany's back five against the Czech Republic in the final of Euro 96 at Wembley.

Offside Trap

More commonly used in the English game, where there are few sweepers, the offside trap is generally unpopular with spectators. From a defender's point of view, however, a perfectly operated trap is a thing of beauty. Some forwards can be caught over and over again.

There are two methods. One is to step up as a single unit as the ball is about to be played forwards. This will usually catch forwards in offside positions, and if it does not at least it forces them to move away from the goal. It is most commonly performed when an attack has been temporarily repulsed, or a corner cleared. It can be played at free-kicks, but the organization needs to be good.

The other system is to hold a line and not be drawn into following a forward who makes a run behind the defence. This is the method Arsenal used under George Graham, though Gunners' captain Tony Adams once insisted 'we don't play an offside trap, it's not our fault if a forward makes a silly run'.

Communication and understanding are the essential components of a successful offside. Most teams use one of the centre-halves to call, or hold the line. The full-backs take their cue from him.

Recent rule changes have made offside more risky. A defence may step up and leave a player offside only to find he is judged not to be interfering with play. Thus defenders and midfielders must watch for runners coming from deep. When stepping up after a cleared corner, take care to go with your man rather than rush out regardless.

It can also be a risky tactic in junior football, where a referee is either by himself or with unqualified, and possibly biased, assistants.

Support Play in Possession

Defenders do most of their work without the ball but, increasingly, they need to be able to play with it as well. Most Continental defenders already can. As teams look to build attacks rather than just hoof the ball forwards, defenders have had to develop better passing skills.

Defenders usually take possession from the goalkeeper or a wayward opposition pass. The cardinal rule is to avoid losing possession in a dangerous area – if in doubt, boot it out. Do not try and dribble past a forward who is pressurizing you, do not pass square in front of your own goal.

When a fellow defender is in possession, drop back at an angle to give him a passing option.

Full-backs can give good support on the flanks. An overlapping run can often find space outside the opposing full-back. Central defenders, especially sweepers, can sometimes find and create space by simply advancing with the ball into midfield.

When a defender moves forward, a team-mate should be ready to cover his position. The defender, meanwhile, should aim to be positive. An overlapping full-back should be looking to shoot or cross rather than dribble. A bad dribble, unlike most bad shots or crosses, allows the opposition to

attack immediately down their own newly exposed flank. For the same reasons a central defender should be looking to shoot or pass.

Goalkeepers

Goalkeeper may seem an isolated position but it is part of the defensive unit. Communication between a goalkeeper and his defenders is vital. Each must have confidence in the other.

Goalkeepers used to just keep goal, now they are sweepers and playmakers as well. Although Bruce Grobbelaar's excursions out of his area are better remembered, Tommy Lawrence was Liverpool's first goalkeeper-sweeper two decades earlier. With the defence pushed up, it was his job to clear long balls played behind or over the defence.

The goalkeeper can also start an attack with his clearance. Full-backs, in particular, should be ready to receive the ball as soon as the keeper has it under control.

An alert goalkeeper sweeps up an attacker's through ball.

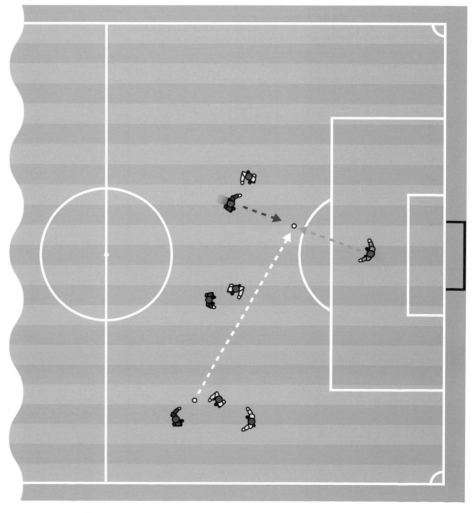

Midfield

The engine room, the nerve centre, the heartbeat – pick your cliché, they are all broadly true. Midfield is where games are won and lost. It does not matter how good your centre-forward is, if he does not get service he cannot score. The midfield's job is to provide that service – and cut the supply to the opposition's goalscorers.

Midfields, like midfielders, are many and varied. They come in different shapes, different sizes and different styles. David Batty and Matt Le Tissier are both midfielders, but that is where the resemblance ends. Batty is primarily a ball-winner, a tackler. He can pass very tidily but defence-splitting through balls are almost as rare as his goals. He has excellent positional discipline and makes a fine holding midfielder, sitting in front of the defence, breaking up attacks.

Le Tissier tackles when he feels like it and does not do it very well. He can go 'missing', taking up positions where he is hard to find and letting opponents brush past him. But he is as good a passer as there is in England, possibly Europe. Short passes, long passes, chipped, curled or driven passes, all appear to come naturally to him. Around the box, he is as good a finisher as any centre-forward.

So who is the better player? That's a matter of perspective. One thing is sure. A midfield full of Battys would no more win a championship than one full of Le Tissiers. A balance is required and, unless you have a team of Bryan Robsons, that will only be achieved by blending the Battys and the Le Tissiers.

The best way of utilizing those particular talents would be to play the diamond midfield. Batty would take up the holding position, Le Tissier the forward one (in the 'hole') and there would be a player either side providing width and ballast.

With other players, a line midfield as used by Manchester United in the mid-1990s may be preferred. They had Roy Keane and Paul Ince (then Roy Keane and Nicky Butt) in the

Two midfields, both 4-4-2: the diamond and the four-in-a-line.

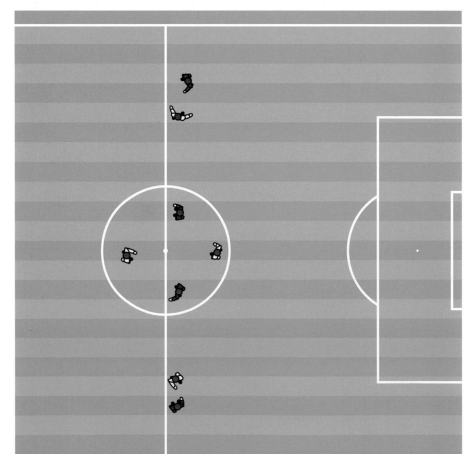

Right: David Platt, a regular goalscorer with his late runs from midfield.

Attack

Remember Germany's first goal of Euro 96? It was against the Czech Republic at Old Trafford. Christian Ziege, the left wing-back, attacked down that flank and laid the ball inside to Thomas Helmer, who fed Fredi Bobic on the edge of the area while Ziege continued his run. Ziege cut inside and, as he drifted across Bobic, the ball was passed on. He stepped past two defenders, wrong-footing them and giving him time to drill the ball just inside the post.

Below: Hard work for any forward, even the greatest – the 4-5-1 formation.

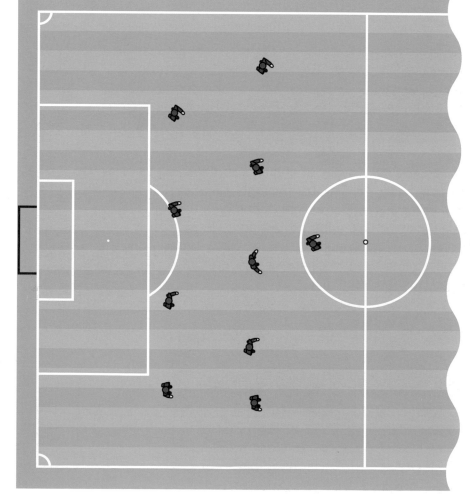

A good goal? Yes, especially if you were the German coach, Berti Voghts, for after the game (which Germany won 2–0) he admitted that the apparently spontaneous move had been worked out in advance on the training ground. Such is the level of planning required these days to outwit modern defences.

Some teams pump the ball at a target man and feed on the nod-downs, some rely on their wing men, others seek to pass their way, one-touch, through the centre. All, however, attack with a pattern. The best teams have several.

In basic terms there are two ways to attack, quickly or slowly. The quick method is used primarily by counter-attacking sides, usually away from home. The Nottingham Forest team of Stan Collymore and Bryan Roy were a classic example. So, away from home, are Tottenham. Defenders and midfielders are always looking to release Ruel Fox on the wing, Chris Armstrong in the channels, or Teddy Sheringham in the air.

Liverpool, though good at counter-attacking, usually have a slower build up. The ball is passed around by the likes of John Barnes and Jamie Redknapp until they see an opening. However, they also have Steve McManaman's dribbling and Patrick Berger's runs to provide a different dimension. Foreign sides, especially from Latin countries, often appear slower still but, once the ball has been passed into a dangerous position, they are capable of upping the tempo very quickly.

Jurgen Klinsmann, a centre-forward with everything — movement, balance, finishing, good feet and heading ability too.

Attacking Formations

As we have seen, teams once played with two wingers, two inside-forwards and a centre-forward. Traditionally these were, respectively, nippy, scheming, and a battering-ram.

Modern attacks are more varied. No one plays with five up – except perhaps Tottenham under Ossie Ardiles when they fielded the Polo formation, the one with the hole in the middle (5-0-5).

Some teams attack with four but the wide men, like Blackburn's Jason Wilcox and Stuart Ripley, will often have some defensive duties in such a formation. Few wingers are given total licence to attack these days; even David Ginola was given a semi-defensive role by Newcastle at one stage.

The central attack can be a sole forward, twin strikers, or split strikers. Occasionally, a team will play three such forwards but they usually get in each others' way, so this is usually only tried when a team is desperately searching for an equalizer. Few British teams, unless they are up against superior opposition, will play a solitary forward because he is usually so outnumbered as to be ineffectual.

Twin strikers are often based on the classic 'one big, one small' pairing, such as Kevin Keegan and John Toshack at Liverpool in the 1970s. Each had complementing strengths. There is less of a disparity in the partnership of Alan Shearer and Les Ferdinand at Newcastle. Ferdinand does more work around the box while Shearer stays closer to it.

Previously, Shearer had a split-striker partnership with Chris Sutton, who played deeper, foraging for Shearer. Teddy Sheringham played in a similar position with Shearer in Euro 96 but with more creative input into the attacking process. These players can be hard to mark because they play deeper than the average central defender but not so deep as to be picked up by the opposing midfield.

The same principle applies to playing 'in the hole', as Eric Cantona did in Europe with his Manchester United team-mates Andy Cole and Ole Gunnar Solskjaer as twin strikers.

After Shearer's departure, and that of Ray Harford, Blackburn adopted a three-striker formation in which Sutton played between two wingers, Wilcox and Kevin Gallagher. This pattern, similar to the Ajax front three (though not their team as a whole) has a lot of width but places responsibility on central midfielders to get forward and feed off Sutton.

Each system has its advantages and disadvantages. Choosing one is often a case of playing to your players' strengths – and the opposition's weaknesses. Whichever is used, certain principles hold true – forwards have to create space, and be given service by their team-mates.

Creating Space

There are two ways of creating space – through skill, or movement. We have previously looked at the skills, like turning and dribbling; this section is about movement.

Split-strikers – one forward as the focal point, the other as the link with midfield.

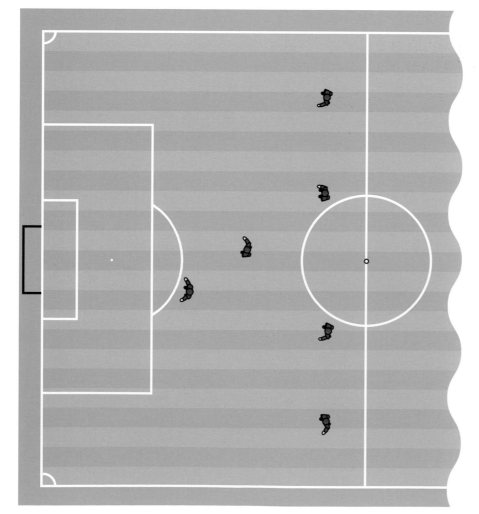

Right: Two wingers and a central striker – the Ajax way. This formation creates width but places great responsibility on the midfield support.

Below right: Two up and one 'in the hole'. This attacking formation was used to devastating effect by Manchester United in their European Cup tie against Oporto at Old Trafford.

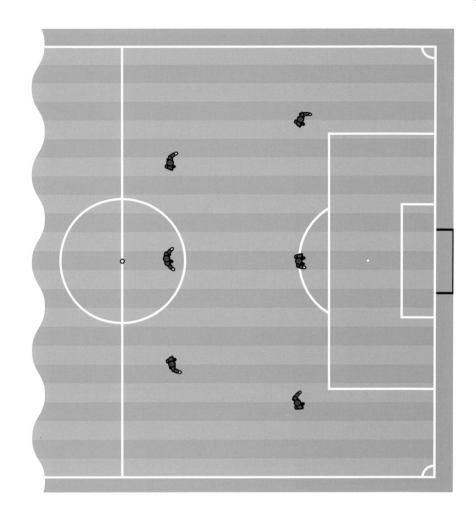

The reasoning is obvious. A player on the move is much harder to mark than one standing still. However, it is not just a matter of moving, it is also a case of where and when. Angled runs ask more and harder questions of defenders, questions like 'Can I afford to go with him and leave my area of responsibility?' They can also drag markers into areas in which they are uncomfortable, such as luring a big strapping centre-half to the wing.

One basic move is to come towards the man on the ball. The marker has to decide whether to come with you, and thus leave a space behind for someone to run into, or let you go and be free to receive the ball and turn. Or a wide player can drift inside – if the full-back goes with him, there will be a space left on the flank for his own full-back to exploit; if he does not, the wide player may be unmarked. Alternatively a central player – or both of them – can go wide, thus creating space for midfielders like David Platt or Robbie Earle to run into. Cantona can often be seen heading for the touchline, defender in tow, and pointing over his shoulder, indicating the pass should be played inside, to Solskjaer, or a breaking midfielder like Nicky Butt.

These manoeuvres are especially successful against teams whose midfielders are bad at picking up players. In such cases defenders can be isolated and outnumbered in certain areas of the field.

As the ball gets nearer the penalty area the movement has to be sharper and later. Jurgen Klinsmann was a master at feinting to move one way then darting off in a different direction. Or you can check your run, then pick it up again. Both moves can wrong-foot the defender and create that precious half-yard of space.

One other example of movement is to run around a team-mate in possession. David

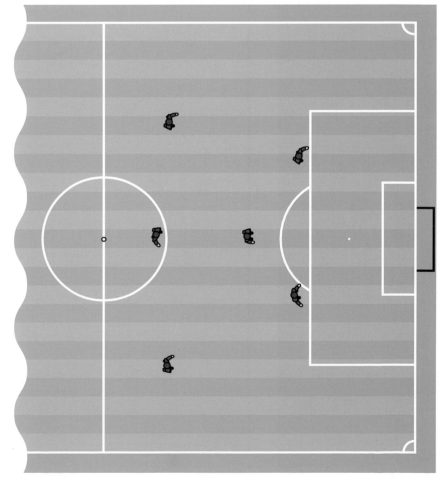

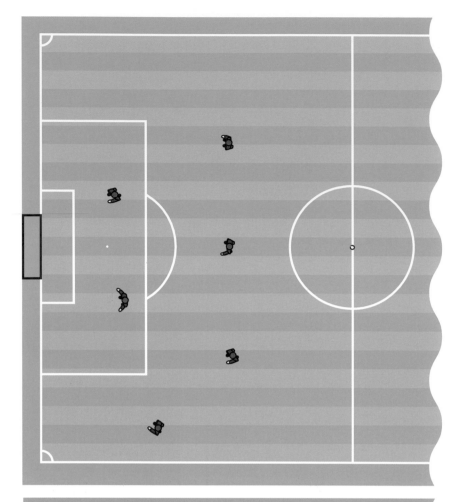

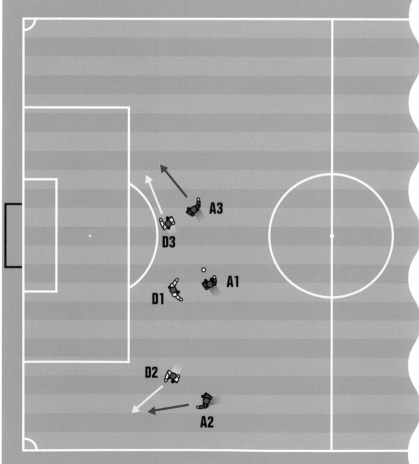

Beckham did this brilliantly for Manchester United against Fenerbahce in Istanbul in 1996. He and Solskjaer had a two-on-two on a counter-attack. As Solskjaer went forward, Beckham ran diagonally behind him, making an overlap. The Norwegian slipped the ball through and Beckham scored. The move was slightly similar to the cross-over, when two players run towards each other and pass over the ball as they pass, causing confusion and delay for defenders.

Such a movement has to be carefully judged – getting too close to team-mates usually makes the opposition's job easier. Also, be careful not to drift offside.

Supply

It does not matter whether your centre-forward is Alan Shearer or Robbie Fowler, if you do not get the ball to him he will not score. Forwards need to be supplied with ammunition. Here are a few ways of getting the ball through to him.

Channel balls

A much-abused technique, this does not just mean lumping the ball into the corners and chasing it. It can do – Jack Charlton encouraged his Irish team to turn defenders around in such a way and John Beck, when managing Cambridge, even went so far as to 'doctor' the corners with sand so the ball held up.

The ball can also be played precisely, whether in the air or along the ground, to open up defences. Seek to pass between defenders – there is often a gap between central defenders and full-backs, occasionally between centre-backs. Teams with wing-backs will often leave space on the flanks.

Played from the centre the ball can be hit diagonally towards the flanks for wide players to run onto, or slid down the centre for a forward's angled run. Juventus, in their matches against Manchester United in

Top left: Two strikers supported by a winger – a common 1970s formation.

Bottom left: Strikers create space for the man on the ball by moving away.

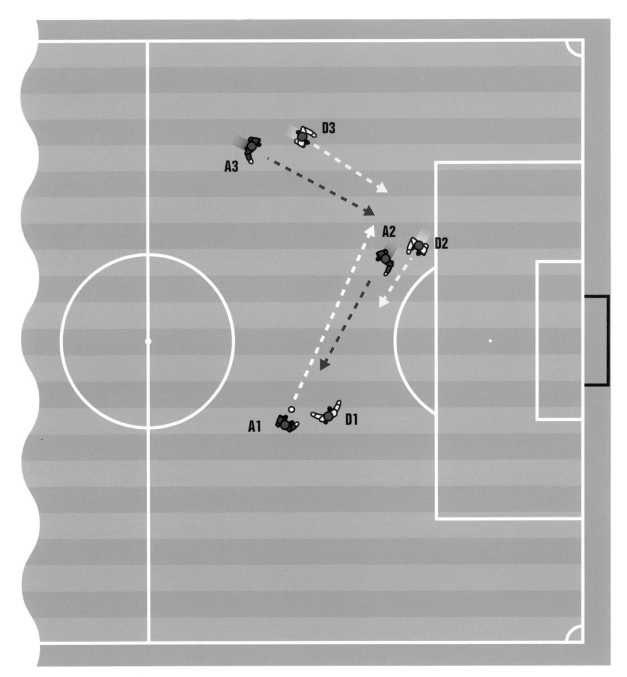

Left: A2's run draws D2 with him, leaving space for A3 to run into. A1 then passes to A3 who has got himself goalside of D3 and in a position to score.

1996/7, gave textbook examples of such passing and movement. From the flanks the ball can be played behind the central defence for a forward's direct run.

Short passing combinations

Channel balls tend to be less successful at international and European level because they can often be picked off by sweepers. The accent on the Continent is often on short passing combinations. The simplest – and still the best – of these is the one-two, or wall-pass.

The player in possession, faced with an opponent, plays the ball diagonally forward to a marked team-mate. He immediately sprints past his opponent and takes up a position where he can receive the ball back. Though his team-mate is marked, he has only to make sure he gets to the ball first to lay it off.

The double pass is an extended variation of this movement. Having played the ball back, the marked man continues his turn to spin off his man and move forward himself. The passer then puts the ball through to him again.

Alternatively, he could play the ball to someone else who has been able to take advantage of this movement to find space elsewhere.

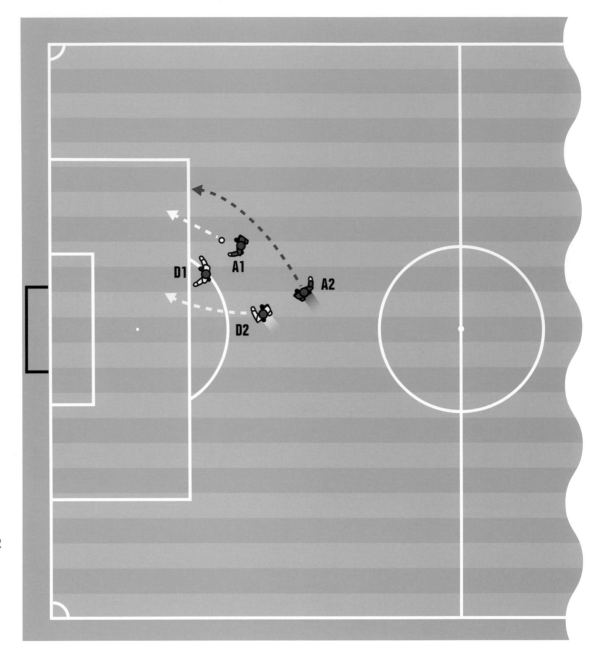

Right: **A common Manchester United move: A2 finds space by going round A1. If D2 follows A2, he will find himself on the wrong side. A better move is to go behind D1 to cover.**

Crosses

The bread and butter of the British game and a major provider of goals. The variations are, if not infinite, certainly many. Back post, near post, penalty spot, low, high, from the byline, from deep. All potentially dangerous.

Where to cross from

Traditionally, wingers have sought to get to the byline before crossing the ball. This was rather easier in Sir Stanley Matthews' day when there would often be one defender trying to stop you. Nowadays they come at wingers in pairs and the temptation is to get the ball over early. This, however, risks offside.

This temptation does not have to be resisted. While the ball pulled back from the byline is a deadly one, it is better to have a cross from a deeper position than no cross at all. Many players, such as David Ginola, only need a sight of the area to whip a cross in. They do not even need to slow the attack by attempting to dribble past the defender.

However, if they do get by the defender, they draw another man out of the goal area and create space. They also draw the goalkeeper to the front post to guard against a shot. This may create a heading chance at the far post, if they can chip the ball over, or a shooting one near the penalty spot from a pull-back.

Where to cross to

The hardest ball to defend is the one behind defenders, causing them to turn. Forwards, running onto it, need only the slightest touch to send the ball goalwards. Not that the ball is fussy – it is quite happy to go in off a slight touch from a defender. Thus defenders have to make good contact to ensure they clear such a cross.

Such a ball is usually crossed from about 10–20 yards out. It needs pace, and accuracy. Pace creates more powerful headers and tricky deflections. The nearer the cross is hit to the goalkeeper the more pace it needs to have. Ideally it should be curled away from the keeper, though perhaps hit close enough to lure him out, and onto the head of an on-rushing

Alan Shearer and Les Ferdinand – similar players but a handful to try to defend against.

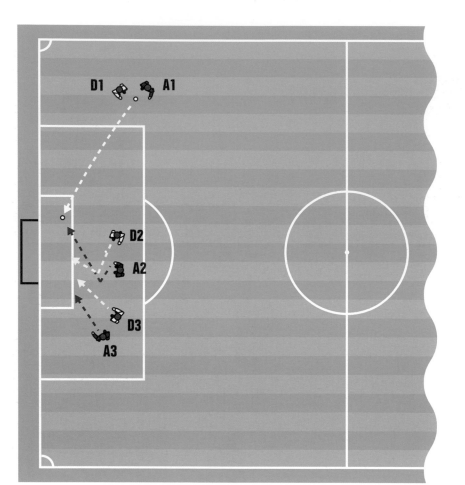

To meet this attacking cross, A2 loses his marker with a feint and heads for the near post, while A3 heads for the far post.

Opposite: Darren Anderton playing the ball into the penalty box in England's draw with Switzerland in Euro 96.

centre-forward. In late 1995 Ginola and Les Ferdinand did this perfectly. Then defenders started to get closer to Ginola, forcing him to cross from deeper positions, and the supply was reduced.

If possible, look for the positions of forwards and goalkeeper before crossing. If the keeper is at the near post, try to hit someone at the far post, and vice versa. Cantona's second goal in Vienna in December 1996 was tapped in at the far post after Beckham, crossing from a deep position on the right, saw him pull away, unnoticed, to the far post and curled his cross behind the defenders. However, unless there is an obvious possibility, it is better to cross to the near or far post than delay. It is up to attackers to get into those areas. Jason McAteer is a fine example of a player who gets the ball in early.

If a player has got to the byline and cut in, he is more likely to create a goal by pulling the ball back along the ground to an oncoming midfielder, or an attacker who has pulled away. If there is no one to pick out, a low cross driven into the six-yard

box can pay dividends as a deflection could go in.

Meeting a Cross

Meeting a cross is like going to a party – go early and you will be hanging around waiting for things to happen. You will also be lumbered with the party bore, in this case a defender. Time your run to meet the ball, that way you are less likely to be marked and will gain maximum height from a jump. A quick feint can help lose a marker – move away from the ball first so you can attack it while the defender is still readjusting.

Where two or more forwards are going into the box, they should be looking to attack different areas. Crossing over will create more space for each other. This needs experience of playing together, or at least good communication.

Switching Play

When an attack is building, be aware of the whole pitch. There are times when a crossfield ball can open up large areas of space to be exploited. Before making such a pass, be sure there is no chance of an interception.

Beating the Offside Trap

Though some linesmen (sorry, referee's assistants) seem slow to catch on, the changes in the offside rule have considerably benefited forwards. Yet a well-drilled offside trap can still be difficult for forwards to beat.

There are three main methods. The most popular is the well-timed through ball, usually aerial. This is best played from the flanks to the centre, or vice versa. Short passes, fed through for a forward-running midfielder, have become far more dangerous since referees began distinguishing between who is interfering with play and who is not.

The one-two is another way of springing the trap and one infrequently used. Even rarer is the dribble. As defenders push up, an opponent, instead of playing the ball in, can sometimes step against the flow and dribble into the area being vacated by the defence.

Set Plays

The following offer opportunities for a team to use well-honed ploys, both basic and complex, to deceive its opposition.

Kick-off

Unlike chess, or even rugby, there are no obvious set plays from the kick-off. However, goals have been scored direct from the start, so it may be worth seeing if the opposition goalkeeper is concentrating. Be careful, too, that your own team is – remember England going 1–0 down to San Marino within seconds of the start of a World Cup qualifier. That quickly scored goal is potentially ruinous for any opposition.

Most teams like to pass the ball about at the start to give players, especially the goalkeeper, an early touch. It also invites opposition players forward, creating space to attack in.

When the centre is a restart, after a goal has been conceded, there is justification in launching a quick attack because the opposition will be feeling jubilant and relaxed. Don't try and dribble through, but look to get players forward quickly into untenanted areas and hit them with early balls.

Corner

These are worth practising; some professional teams spend hours on their corner drills, offensively and defensively.

Defending teams should have a man on each post, one forward of the near post, watching for the near post flick, and have every man marked. Two players should go out for short corners; one defender will be outnumbered. It is sometimes worth stationing a player ten yards from the kicker to cut out some crosses and generally put him off. This has to be weighed against the loss of a player in the box. The same applies to bringing back forwards. It is worth leaving at least one player up as an outlet, because he will have to be marked.

Attacking teams have three main options: the near post, the six-yard box, and the short corner. One other alternative is the pull back to the edge of the box. These should be mixed up to keep opponents guessing.

The near-post corner is looking to be flicked on. This late change in trajectory makes it difficult for goalkeepers and defenders to clear. Alan Shearer's goal against Germany in Euro 96, flicked on by Tony Adams, was a classic example. In these situations, winning the second ball is crucial.

Some teams prefer to hit fast inswingers, or outswingers, into the six-yard box for a direct goal attempt. Duncan Ferguson's ability to get on the end of such corners from Andy Hinchcliffe was a potent weapon for Everton.

The inswinging corner.

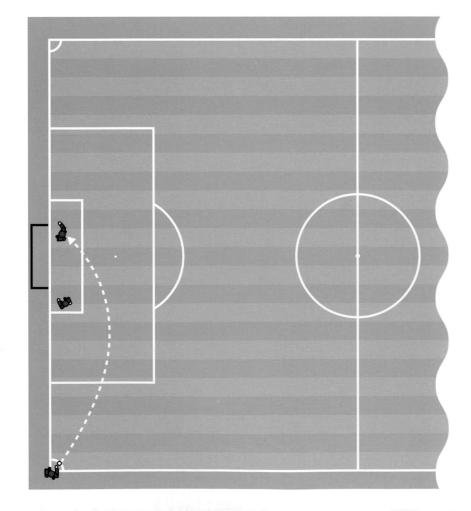

The short corner has two purposes: it changes the angle of approach and gives forwards a second chance to lose their markers in the area. Care should be taken that the defence does not implement the offside trap.

Attackers should be looking to gain a yard of space through feints and late movement as the ball is crossed. Watch Shearer in the aforementioned goal. Note the way he and Teddy Sheringham took up similar positions; one German found himself marking both. As Shearer made his move, Sheringham baulked the marker.

Some teams will put a man on the goalkeeper. Jack Charlton always stood there for Leeds. The defence need to mark this man and keep him away from the keeper. As in so many areas of the pitch, courage can be as important as ability in winning the ball at corners.

One other possibility, more often seen on the Continent, is to pull the ball back to a player waiting on the edge of the area to volley. This is very difficult but Ronald Koeman, the Dutch defender, made it a feature of his play.

Above right: An inswinging corner for a back post runner.

Right: A corner hit to the edge of the box for a shot or cross.

Below: A short corner to change the angle.

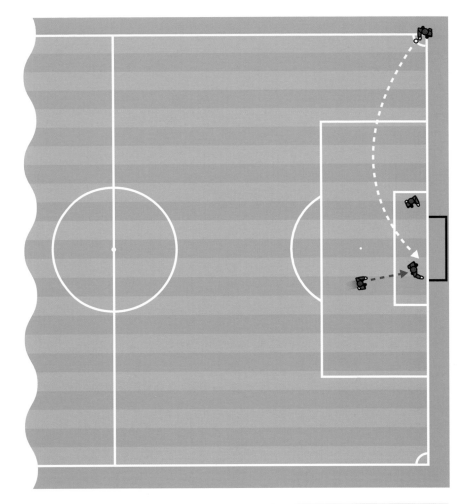

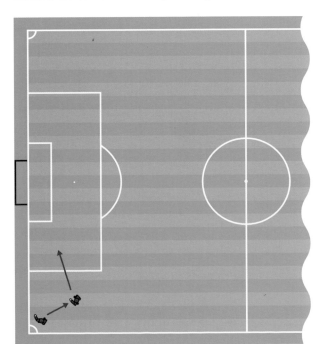

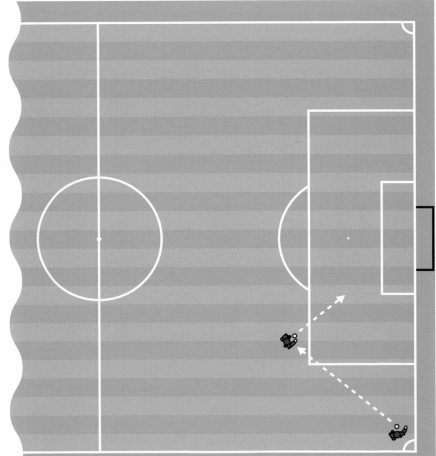

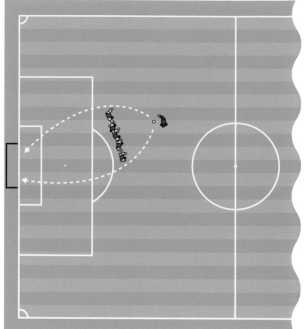

Above: A direct shot from a free-kick.

Gary Neville's long throws give Manchester United an extra attacking weapon.

Throw-in

In some hands the long throw is almost as good as a corner. Andy Legg, Birmingham's Welsh international, has the longest throw around, but Gary Neville and Vinnie Jones are other exponents. Attacking teams are usually looking for a flick-on from a throw-in because of the difficulty in matching the pace of a corner.

Elsewhere throws need to be taken quickly, before team-mates are marked up. If in doubt, a ball down the line will often gain ground. This is always preferable to a risky throw into the middle if the throw is in your own half.

Free-kick

For a free-kick more than 35 yards from goal the choice is either to 'put it in the mixer' (i.e. pump the ball forward towards a cluster of players on the edge of the area), or pass it short, keep possession, and build an attack as in open play.

A free-kick within shooting range opens up a lot more possibilities. On the flanks it is effectively a corner from a different angle with the bonus, if it is direct, of being a shooting chance. Around the 'D' it offers a good opportunity to score, whether direct or indirect (in which case it will need to be tapped before shooting).

Most teams, at all levels, shoot in these situations. The likes of Stuart Pearce, Alan Shearer and Gary McAllister have scored many goals from free-kicks.

The usual intention is to bend the ball around, or over, the wall, dipping it into one of the corners with pace. Some teams station a mini-wall in front of the kicker to disguise his intention; some lay the ball square to an unexpected kicker, where generally the procedure is no more elaborate than a left-footed kicker running over the ball before a right-footed one hits it (or vice versa).

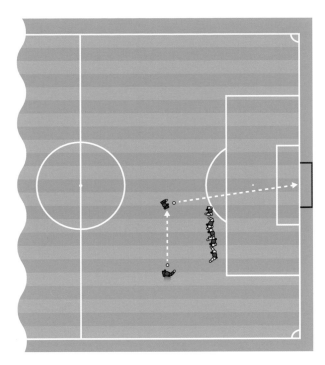

A trapped free-kick can offer a clear view of goal.

This free-kick is crossed in for the forwards to attack.

A free-kick down the line to an overlapping team-mate creates a good angle for attacking the goal.

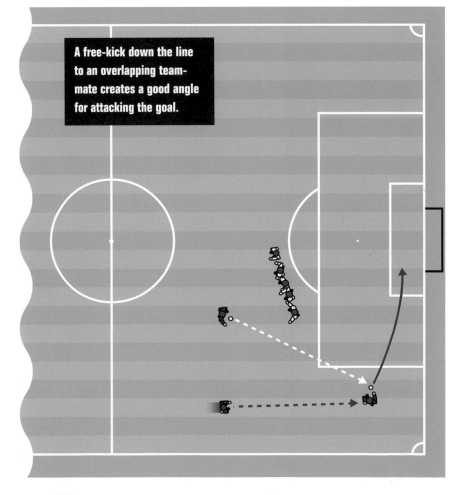

One variation seen in Euro 96 was the low free-kick driven under the wall. This followed the growing tendency of walls to jump in unison as the kick was taken, leaving a gap underneath. The Dutch used this technique against Scotland; Andy Goram saved.

As shooting has improved, and balls become more prone to movement, general inventiveness at free-kicks has declined. The days of Willie Carr and Ernie Hunt's outlawed 'donkey-drop' kick (one flicking the ball up between his legs for the other to volley) seem long gone.

There have been some similar attempts. Carr's memory was revived in 1995/6 with a series of 'scooped' free-kicks setting up volleys; England, against Hungary, scored from a neat quick free-kick; some players chip free-kicks over walls for team-mates to run onto.

Less common is the wall-pass with the wall – or, rather, a team-mate standing in it. Unsurprising really, as this is very difficult, but it can catch a lot of defenders out.

Defenders hate having forwards in the wall. It can lead to plenty of distracting pushing and shoving while they ensure that, should the forward step away at the last

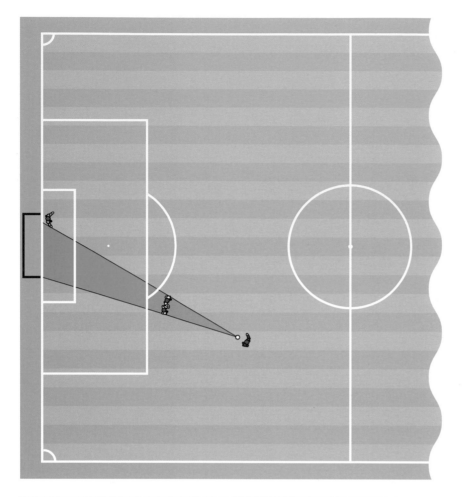

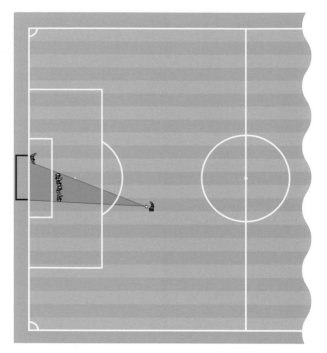

The wall: How many players a defence has in the wall will depend on distance, the reputation of the shooter and the goalkeepers's preference.

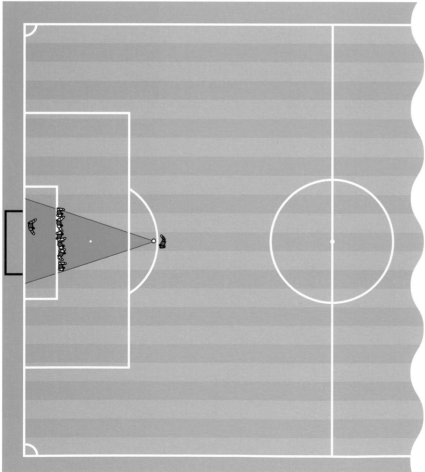

moment, a hole will not be left. This is the cardinal sin. A wall, once constructed – and a defender should quickly stand over the ball when a free-kick is awarded to prevent it being taken quickly – should not have gaps. Most teams will delegate a runner, someone to sprint out early and try and charge down the kick, but this player should come from the edge of the wall, not its heart.

Goalkeepers decide the number of players in the wall, two for a kick 35–40 yards out (and only then if a noted shot is taking it) to up to seven on the edge of the 'D' – while taking account of the need to mark. Most goalkeepers station a wall to guard one corner of the goal while they take up a position close to the other, giving them scope to get across to a gently flighted chip to the other post. Care should be taken over who stands in the wall. Defenders should be busy defending, while the braver forwards get in the wall.

Penalty

Penalty kicks are about nerve first and technique second. How often have you seen the most famous player being the one who misses in the penalty shoot-out? From Liam

Brady and Mario Kempes in 1981, to Roberto Baggio in 1994, the best technicians have often failed to keep their nerve.

Though there are variations (John Aldridge's stutter and Dwight Yorke's chip come to mind), most players choose to run up steadily then blast or place. Both Ray Stewart and his successor as West Ham's penalty taker, Julian Dicks, were blasters. John Robertson, one of the coolest takers ever, was a placer, aiming low and just inside the base of the post – the hardest place for a goalkeeper to get down to. Matt Le Tissier, who has the best contemporary penalty record, is another placer but with pace.

For goalkeepers the penalty offers a chance of glory. No one expects a save.

Some keepers go early, others wait. There are arguments for both. Go early and you might be lucky: the ball could be blasted at you. Wait and it may be hit straight at you, or close enough to react to. It is a matter of preference.

Paul Cooper, the Ipswich goalkeeper in the late 1970s and early 1980s, had a tremendous record of saving penalties. He used to stand to one side of the goal, inviting the forward to hit into the larger space, then get across to save it. David Seaman tends to watch the kicker carefully and react as he hits it.

Both defenders and attackers should be ready to follow up for a rebound. The key areas are just inside either post, or in the middle of the goal.

Dean Holdsworth is in the centre of a Wimbledon wall facing Stuart Pearce's feared left foot.

The Laws
of the Game

The laws of the game, which are relatively simple, were first codified in 1848. They were drawn up by representatives of the public schools, the first exponents of organized football. Until then each school or club had its own rules, which included catching the ball and running with it (the precursor to rugby), throwins with one hand and 'hacking' (deliberately kicking players on the shin).

These rules were gradually adapted until, in 1863, the newly formed Football Association adopted a set of laws drawn up by Cambridge University.

In the early years there were a number of changes – the introduction of the crossbar, handling being restricted to the goalkeeper, the elimination of 'tries and conversions' until, by the 1880s, the game became recognizably similar to today's.

Minor changes have continued, most notably after the sterile World Cup of 1990. They include the banning of back-passes to goalkeepers, a 'tickling' of the offside law and a new interpretation of serious foul play.

More changes could follow, driven as much by the need to cater for television interests as the desire to improve the game.

Laws, incidentally, are determined by the International Board. For historical reasons, this consists of the four home nations, England, Scotland, Wales and Northern Ireland, and four rotating representatives of the other 150-plus countries in FIFA, the game's overall governing body. The desire to retain this format is one reason why Great Britain does not enter the Olympic football competition; such a step may lead to the four Football Associations having to combine.

What follows is a précis of the 17 Laws and associated advice. For more detailed regulations, and interpretations, I recommend the FA's *Laws of the Football Association – Guide for Players and Referees*, updated annually.

Note: All or some of Laws I, II, III, VII can be amended for matches involving players under 16, veterans (over 35) and women.

The field of play

The pitch is rectangular in shape with the length between 100 and 130 yards, the width between 50 and 100. A half-way line shall be marked with a circle of 10 yards radius at its centre. Most professional grounds are about 115 × 75 yards.

The goal area, 20 yards by 6 yards, extends form the goal-line and is enclosed within the penalty area, a 44-yard by 18-yard rectangle. Within that area, 12 yards from the goaline and in line with the centre of the goal, is the penalty spot. An arc, radius 10 yards, should be drawn outside the circle.

Each of the four corners should have a flag of at least 5 ft. in height placed on it and a quarter circle, with a radius of one yard, drawn around it.

The goal consists of two upright posts 8 yards apart and topped with a bar 8 ft. in height. The goals should be anchored to the ground and have nets attached. If the crossbar breaks during a competitive match the game cannot be resumed until the bar has been replaced. In a friendly match, a rope is permitted, or nothing at all, goals to be judged by the referee. (See the Field of Play diagram on page 96.)

The ball

The ball should be spherical with a weight of 14–16 oz, a circumference of 27–28 in. and a pressure of 0.6–1.1 atm.

If the ball bursts or becomes deflated during play the match shall be restarted with a dropped ball at the point at which the ball became defective unless it was in the goal area. In such cases the restart will be on the edge of the goal area, parallel to the goal-line.

Number of players

Teams will consist of no more than 11 players, one of whom will be the goalkeeper. There can be up to five substitutes, none of whom can enter the field until the departing player has left and without the referee's permission. They should come on at the half-way line.

If one team has, or is reduced to less than seven players, the match should not be considered valid. If a player is sent off before a match begns, he may be replaced but only by a designated substitute.

Players' equipment

A player shall wear a jersey, shorts, socks, boots and shinpads; these last-mentioned must be covered by socks. The goalkeeper shall wear a jersey of a different colour.

Referees

The referee's authority begins as soon as he enters the field of play. His decision is final. He should enforce the laws, playing advantage when appropriate, record events in the game and keep time. He can stop or suspend the game whenever he deems necessary, signal the recommencement after any stoppage.

To win the respect of players, he should understand every law, be absolutely fair and impartial, and keep physically fit.

> **Football is a gentlemen's game played by hooligans, and rugby a hooligan's game played by gentlemen.**
>
> **Anon, 19th century**

Referee's assistants

The referee's assistant shall indicate when the ball is out of play; which side is entitled to the subsequent corner-kick, goal-kick or throw-in; and when a substution is to be made.

In practice, assistants also signal offside and infringements the referee may not have seen.

Duration of the game

Two periods of 90 minutes plus injury time, to be added at the end of each respective half, to make up for time lost through substitutions, injuries and time-wasting. The amount is down to the referee's discretion.

The start of play

The choice of ends and kick-off will be decided by a toss of a coin. The team winning the toss shall have the option of the choice of ends or kick-off.

Upon the referee's signal the game shall be started by the ball being kicked forward not less than its own circumerence from the centre-spot. Every player shall be in his own half and none of the opposing side within ten metres of the ball. If any of the above are not followed the kick shall be retaken.

The kicker cannot kick the ball again until another player has. If he does, an indirect free-kick shall be given against him.

After a goal is scored the team conceding shall kick off in the same way. After half-time the game will restart with a kick-off taken by a different team from that which started the game.

After any other stoppage which is not caused by an infringement or the ball going out of play the game shall be restarted by the referee dropping the ball at the place of the suspension – unless this is in the goal area. Then the ball shall be dropped on the line marking the goal area parallel to the place of suspension. If the ball is played before it hits the ground the ball shall be dropped again.

Ball in and out of play

The ball is out of play when it is wholly over the goal-line or touch line or when the referee has stopped play.

Method of scoring

A goal is scored when the whole of the ball is passed over the goal-line, under the crossbar and betwen the posts.

A goal cannot be allowed if the ball is stopped by an outside agent from going over the line. In such a case the game will be restarted with a dropped ball. If a spectator comes onto the pitch as the ball is going into goal [as with Geoff Hurst's third in the 1966 World Cup final] the goal shall be allowed unless the spectator has made contact with the ball or otherwise interfered with play. In such cases, a drop ball is taken.

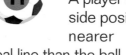

Off-side

A player is in an off-side position if he is nearer to the goal-line than the ball, unless he is (a) in his own half of the field or (b) he is not nearer the goal-line than two of his opponents.

He shall only be declared in an off-side position and penalized if, in the opinion of the referee, he is (a) interfering with play or an opponent or (b) seeking to gain an advantage by being in that position. He cannot be off-side direct from a goal-kick, corner kick or throw-in.

Violent conduct, serious foul play, foul or abusive language or a second cautionable offence incurs a dismissal (red card). Fouling a player who had a clear goal-scoring opportunity is a sending off offence as is handling the ball and preventing a goal (except for the goalkeeper).

A bemused Andre Kanchelskis of Manchester United receives his marching orders for hand ball during the Coca-Cola Cup Final against Aston Villa in 1994.

12 Fouls and misconduct

Nine offences, if committed intentionally, are punished by a direct free-kick (penalty kick if in the penalty area). They are:

- Kicking or attempting to kick an opponent – tripping an opponent
- Jumping at an opponent
- Charging an opponent in a dangerous or violent manner
- Charging an opponent from behind (unless the opponent is obstructing)
- Striking, attempting to strike or spitting at an opponent
- Holding an opponent
- Pushing an opponent
- Handling the ball (except for the goalkeeper in his area)

Five offences are punishable by an indirect free-kick:

- Dangerous play such as raising a foot to the goalkeeper
- Charging when the ball is not in playing distance
- Obstructing an opponent
- Charging the goalkeeper
- As a goalkeeper, taking more than four steps while holding or bouncing the ball, touching the ball with his hands after a deliberate back-pass by a team-mate, or time-wasting.

Entering the field of play without permission, persistant infringement, dissent and ungentlemanly conduct incurs a caution (yellow card) from the referee and, for the last three offences, an indirect free-kick.

Free-kick

A goal can be scored from a direct free-kick but not, without being touched by another player, from an indirect kick. Opponents must be ten yards from the kick and, if it is taken in the defending side's penalty area, the ball must leave the area before another player can touch it. The ball must be stationary. The kicker can only kick it once before another player touches the ball.

Throw-in

A throw-in is taken to restart the game after the ball has gone over the touch-line. The taker, who is in the opposing side to the player who put the ball out, shall face the playing area and, with both feet on the ground, throw the ball with both hands from behind and over his head. Part of each foot shall be behind or on the touchline.

DIRECT FREE KICK
Both the arm and hand are used to show the direction of the kick.

Penalty-kick

A penalty kick is a direct free-kick inside the penalty area. It shall be taken from the penalty mark with all players, save the goalkeeper and taker, outside the area.

The goalkeeper shall not move before it is taken nor other players encroach into the area.

If time has been extended for a penalty to be taken the match, or half, shall be over as soon as the kick is taken. There will not be time to shoot from a rebound.

Goal-kick

When the attacking team put the ball out of play behind the goal-line the game is restarted with a goal kick that may be taken from any point inside the goal area. Opposing players may not be in the area when the kick is taken. The ball may not be played again until it has left the area.

Corner-kick

When the defending team put the ball out of play behind the goal-line the game is restarted with a corner kick. The defending team cannot be within ten yards of the kick. The kicker may not touch the ball twice. A goal can be scored direct from the kick.

> **The trouble with referees is that they know the rules but they don't know the game.**
> **Bill Shankly, manager of Liverpool, 1971**

PLAY ON – ADVANTAGE:
When a referee sees an offence, he
may choose to use the advantage
and indicate that play shall
continue.

SUBSTITUTION:
Signalling to the referee for a
substitution to be made.

INDIRECT FREE KICK:
This signal shall be maintained
until the kick has been taken.

The Field of Play

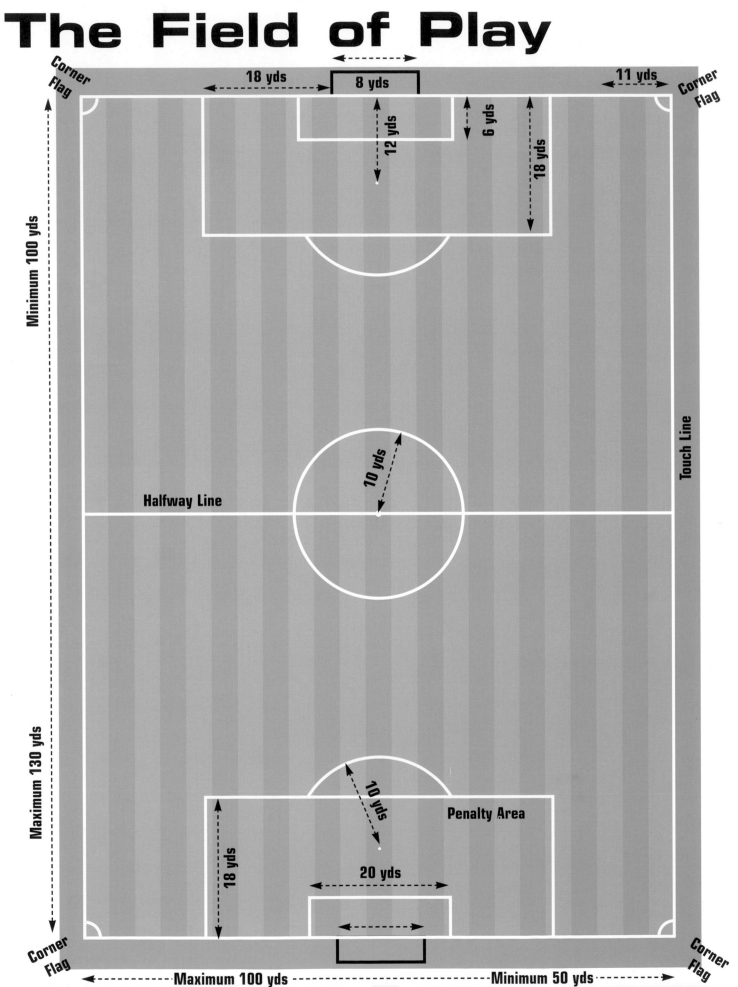

Corner Flag

18 yds

8 yds

11 yds

Corner Flag

12 yds

6 yds

18 yds

Minimum 100 yds

Touch Line

10 yds

Halfway Line

Maximum 130 yds

10 yds

Penalty Area

18 yds

20 yds

Corner Flag

Corner Flag

Maximum 100 yds

Minimum 50 yds